THE
UNHYPHENATED
CANUCK

THE UNHYPHENATED CANUCK

Reflections and Confessions of an Opinionated Immigrant

HERB DUERR

iUniverse, Inc.
New York Lincoln Shanghai

The Unhyphenated Canuck
Reflections and Confessions of an Opinionated Immigrant

iUniverse, Inc.

iUniverse books may be ordered through booksellers or by contacting:

iUniverse
2021 Pine Lake Road, Suite 100
Lincoln, NE 68512
www.iuniverse.com
1-800-Authors (1-800-288-4677)

The views expressed in this work are solely those of the author and do not necessarily reflect the views of the publisher, and the publisher hereby disclaims any responsibility for them.

ISBN-13: 978-0-595-42819-9 (pbk)
ISBN-13: 978-0-595-87157-5 (ebk)
ISBN-10: 0-595-42819-3 (pbk)
ISBN-10: 0-595-87157-7 (ebk)

Printed in the United States of America

I have indeed enjoyed a wonderful life.
If it started all over again
there is nothing of real significance
that I would want to do differently.

For Gussie, my spouse of over fifty years;
our son Kenneth, who really made us a family;
his wife Birte, who became one of us;
and our Grandchildren Steven, Kevin and Emma,
who make our circle complete.

CONTENTS

INTRODUCTION

Do I really need a bodyguard? Living dangerously was not what I had in mind, when I consented to bare my soul for an audience broader than my immediate family. Yet even my most contentious observations should not incite such stern reaction. Surely *never in Canada, eh*!

Personal experiences, spanning a period beginning with my arrival as an adolescent in my chosen country, and extending to well beyond my retirement after a lengthy career, form part of these revelations. Where my musings are autobiographical, members of my immediate family appear in various scenarios.

Whenever philosophical, to address a number of often divisive subjects, I might reflect my really "deep thinking", or deliberately become flippant in style or corny in content. Politically correct? Not a chance! Biased from a right-of-centre and law-and-order perspective? But of course!

I address a great variety of topics relating to every-day life; and this is what provides the fodder for disagreement. Taken out of context, some commentary might indeed appear offensive. Yet, this was never my intent and—when *everything* is pursued—it should become obvious, even to an utterly antagonistic reader. Hopefully, therefore, this wider release of my debatable views will not result in house calls from cross-burning rednecks; self-immolating militants with explosive-belts; or gun-toting idols of *gangsta-rap* performers.

Canada had originally been my second choice, as the country in which I would build a new life. But it did not take me long to appreciate my new environment. Although the required sponsorship for entry in the United States of America—my initial target for emigration—became available within a year of my arrival, I no longer wished to move there.

Since becoming a Canadian, I have valued this country, my citizenship, and my civic duties, most sincerely. Unlike some Canadians, particularly among those who were born here, I could never take the freedom and the opportunities offered, and the good fortune that surrounds me, for granted.

As an immigrant, I had made the decision to leave the place that spawned and nurtured me, and to grab a piece of Canada and make it mine. It was a daring choice and a constant struggle, but it proved to have been the right thing to do. And Canada, my country, made me hers. *I am a Canuck!*

My literary endeavours commenced when I was 69 years of age and happily retired. It was my daughter-in-law who persuaded me to compose my memoirs, for the enlightenment of my grandchildren and for the future generations of our family. This I did! In five books to date, I have documented my experiences and views, and never hesitated to reveal my ignorance, folly, or just bloody-mindedness.

These writings may well reflect what I consider the pillars for a successful existence: Throughout one's entire lifetime, the pursuit of *Learning* to indulge an enduring curiosity; during the working years, a *Career* that brings satisfaction and appropriate financial rewards; and, above all, the unconditional *Love* of a happy and supportive family.

Apart from such basic criteria, everything else—especially if it might prove disappointing—could easily become "a giggle", to be totally ignored or assessed with a sense of humour. This is advice, which I freely extend to others but—as one can glean from several of my more dogmatic compositions—I do not always accept.

I would hope that, with this as-I-see-the-world collection, I can provoke some controversy. A measure of such accomplishment would be an abundance of rebuttals from those readers who—when they feel slighted or shocked—become sufficiently aroused to respond. Reproachful censure with perceptive critique might then inspire me to do even more writing!

IMMIGRATION 1951

The absurdity of the Immigration Officer's questioning, as it pertained to my geographic direction into the country, did not occur to me at the time. To his inquiry of "Where do you want to go?" I hinted at Montreal, Toronto, even Hamilton. He told me that these were overrun by new immigrants, and that I should instead choose another place. Following my request for guidance, he referred me to the huge map on his office wall and suggested that I select a destination on my own.

The city of Regina appeared sufficiently distant from where he had discouraged me to settle. It was somewhere in the middle of the country, and it had a nice-sounding name. Unknown to me at the time, it was also in Saskatchewan, the Wheat Province. Yet—to my later great amazement—he accepted this as the chosen destination for Canada's newest prospective lumberjack.

I don't know where this chap was from or how much of a liquid lunch he had imbibed that day. Perhaps he merely demonstrated his peculiar sense of humour to an unsuspecting *Kraut*. Or could it really be that he had never discovered that there were no trees to be harvested in the Regina area?

Crucial was that I obtained my visa as an immigrant; to a country where even native-born Canadians—every single one—are descendants of immigrants. Despite some claims to the contrary, this most certainly includes our Indians and Eskimos or, as they prefer to be called today, our *First Nation* or *Inuit* communities. In the opinion of professed experts, these are the progeny of roving bands arriving over the then existing land-bridge from Asia.

My origins were in Europe. Those ancestors that I was able to authenticate in many years of research came primarily from Germany; with only minor embellishments to the mélange by infiltrators from France and Switzerland. Yet, since the area where I grew up had for centuries been overrun by ethnic groups from throughout Europe and occasionally from Asia, there might well have been other, although undocumented, contributions as well.

My hopes and aspirations were no different, when I decided to leave Germany for Canada in 1951. I, too, sought peace and the possibility of a better life, just like the many thousands who emigrated from post-war Europe during those years.

Conflicts between France and Germany had been going on forever. I felt then that, at some future date, Germans and French would again be at each other's throat. My grandparents' generation had suffered through three major wars (1870–71, 1914–18 and 1939–45). I had enough with just the one clash and did not wish to endure another. I wanted to get out of Europe.

The Canadian Government Immigration Mission in Karlsruhe had an elaborate screening process. They tried to verify that I was politically untarnished by a Nazi past, attested completely healthy, and had no criminal record. Documents submitted with my original application, issued by the authorities of the day following their own investigations, confirmed that I qualified on all three counts.

Then followed the personal interview. Since I did not have a specific trade skill, I was informed that I could only be granted a visa in either the "General Labourer" or the "Lumberjack" categories. I elected to come with the more romantic designation. Albeit—misdirected by the immigration counsellor's ignorance, inebriation or malicious intent—to the wrong part of the country for such employment.

My parents had offered to finance the return passage to Germany, should my Canadian venture not be up to expectations. But they refused to facilitate this audacious undertaking of their only son by funding my initial departure. I therefore had to obtain an Assisted Passage Loan from the Canadian government.

I sailed from Bremerhaven aboard the *Castelbianco* of the Italian *SITMAR* Line. We were told that she was a *Victory* Ship, built as a troop carrier during the war. There were two hundred of us in the one sleeping area, so I was lucky that my bunk was near the fresh air intake. I was more fortunate still, to have two interesting neighbours, one of whom to become a life-long friend.

Meals aboard were plentiful and nourishing. But rough seas reduced the number of participants for each subsequent meal, during part of what—with stops to take on additional passengers in France and England—may have been a ten-day voyage.

We docked in Quebec City on October 24th. Immigration and Customs screening was aboard ship. In antiquated railcars, we traversed northern Ontario on our way to the Prairie Provinces. Occasionally, the train would halt long enough for us to disembark and buy provisions from food outlets near a railway station. There were always much hooting and hollering to get us back aboard when the engineer was ready to leave. For most of the journey, the first—perhaps the only—memorable impression was that there was an immense wilderness area yet to be settled.

Conversations with my newly found buddies revealed that one of them knew a very influential and, hopefully, helpful person in Winnipeg. Yet, my documents destined me to Regina. But why would I want to leave these friends, whose own immigration papers directed them to Winnipeg? I decided, therefore, to disembark at the earlier stop and that harvesting of trees in Regina would have to wait.

My apprehension about possible enforcement of my "lumberjack in Regina" status by the authorities was of short duration. No one seemed to care where I went or what I did. There was no residence registration with police either. This, I surmised, was really a free country, where everyone did his own thing and was left to flourish or famish according to his personal devices, a combination of his skill, effort and, not least, luck.

Temporary accommodation for those newly arrived was provided at the railway facilities in the station area off Winnipeg's Main Street.

Every day and all day, the three of us marched from one company to the other, in search of employment. Since my English was more fluent than the nearly non-existent version of my pals, I became the spokesman. Where we received any encouragement about possible prospects, we reappeared again and again. *Canada Packers* was one of these firms where we became well known to the Personnel Department. They eventually named us "The Three Musketeers".

My very first and extremely short-lived employment in Canada was as a plumber's helper. One of my chums had the gall to persuade the project manager on a construction site that he was a qualified plumber. He—and I as his accredited helper—spent all day moving water pipes this way and that, without making any of the required installations. Our lack of talent and experience had become obvious when, by the end of the day, we were fired—with pay for our eight hours of "work". It was probably the last time for this contractor to employ any one of "*them there* bloody *DPs*".

DP, which stood for *Displaced Person,* was a term the locals applied in a somewhat derogatory fashion to recent immigrants from the war-torn Europe of the time. Explanations that a *DP* was someone without a country, who could not or did not want to return to his native soil—usually in Eastern Europe—were of no interest. Although we still had a homeland and were "real" immigrants—not refugees—*DPs* we were labelled. All of us!

With a German family name, and most certainly a German accent, our designation from some might even have been "Nazi". But never to our faces!

My buddies and I finally succeeded in locating the "influential" contact. While he did not turn out as a *Mr. Winnipeg*—the allegedly well-established *mover and shaker*—he certainly proved very considerate. He spent the good part of a day driving us around to a number of his mates. And it was at *Litz the Mover* that one of his acquaintances from Winnipeg's German Club employed the three of us immediately.

For 90 cents an hour we worked during the daytime at levelling huge oil tanks in a refinery storage yard. I operated a pneumatic drill to break the frozen ground in the coldest temperatures that I had ever experienced. For these outdoor assignments, I wore various layers of much of the clothing that I possessed.

Still working until late at night after regular hours, we earned overtime pay and, at $1.35 per hour, moved heavy factory and office equipment, including bank safes. A weekend project was the transfer of an entire residential building from one site to another.

To move into our own quarters, my friends and I rented a furnished place at 720 Broadway Avenue. This was a rather magnificent name for a street with not very glamorous rooming houses. We had one bedroom with an adjoining kitchen. The bathroom was shared with a group of young ladies, who occupied similar facilities across the hall from ours, and regularly used up the hot water just ahead of our turn to take a shower. Fortunately, considering our other priorities at that time, we never got to know them really well during the few weeks of our joint residence.

My roommates and I took turns with various household chores. Since I was the first to arrive home in the evening, I usually did the cooking. The other chaps washed the dishes or swept and dusted the place. Shopping for groceries we undertook jointly once each week.

We lived frugally. The evening meal was our main repast for the day and consisted alternately of fried potatoes or noodles, which we served either with scrambled eggs, or pork chops, or sausages. Then the cycle started all over again. Not too much variety with these culinary delights, but easily prepared.

My lunch to take to work usually provided sardines on white bread and an apple. No comments ever from my colleagues about the obvious fishy smell. For breakfast I do not recall what we had, or, indeed, if we ate any. The three of us were already tall enough and didn't need that much food to make us grow, especially not if it cost money.

The employment with *Litz* had to be of short duration. From December onwards, they retained only their regular staff for the winter months. So, again, we were out seeking a new source of income.

I quickly ended up with another temporary assignment, this one at the *T. Eaton Company* for the remainder of their Christmas rush. In their mail-order warehouse, I searched for and usually located parcels addressed to customers from coast to coast. All of us were quite busy for a couple of weeks. As the pace slackened off close to the holidays, the trick to retain continuing employment—at least for a few days—was to appear busy. We accomplished this through one of our colleague's intentional misplacement of a few packages, while the rest of our crew went hunting for them throughout the storage area.

Again, I needed a job. And my next assignment turned out to be the most difficult work I ever had to do, since—despite my brief home-cooking interlude—I lacked both the experience and any talent for the task. I became a Second Cook on *CN Railways'* dining cars. An attraction was, of course, that it provided all the delicious food that I could eat and a bunk to sleep during the journey.

Not once, during those early years of my Canadian working life, did a potential employer view any documentation on my previous assignments; nor did I ever have to present certificates or diplomas about my educational background. The routine seemed to be that you sold yourself as the one best qualified to do the job. If this proved correct, then you continued working; if it did not, you were out on your ear. Of course, should it ever be discovered that you had claimed credits you did not possess, you might be fired as well.

Upon my return to Winnipeg from a business trip—a cooking journey, I should say, this one to Churchill/Manitoba—I was elated to find a letter from the manager of the local branch of a national transportation company. He had responded to one of my written applications to several advertisers in the Help Wanted section of the *Winnipeg Free Press*. He asked me for an interview, I went, he hired me. Now I was an Invoice Typist at $135 per month.

Things were picking up! I had—so I hoped—a permanent job in an office; a boss who was happy with what I was doing and left me to do it; and some really swell fellow workers. I was able to pay off my Assisted Passage Loan to the government and actually save some money. Not bad for a start!

My monthly share of the cost for accommodation was fifteen dollars, and to eat, drink, smoke (at that time I still suffered from this disgusting addiction), and be merry, I allowed an average of one dollar per day. This allocation also covered a movie ticket on each Saturday, as well as a 5-cent ice-cream bar for consumption during the screening. Depending on the type of theatre, the day's admission was between 25 and 35 cents with usually two, sometimes even three, films running in a show. The lengthy walk toward the movie district near Portage and

Main, the centre of town, and the eventual return home, also on foot, saved ten cents each way in streetcar fare.

At that time, in the opinion of the local populace, someone who spoke with an accent (I did then, and still do somewhat now, and who doesn't in the Toronto area, anyway?) could not possibly have any useful educational background. Explaining my *Abitur* as a senior matriculation high school graduation, and relating it convincingly to something Canadian, was an impossible task. I decided, therefore, to acquire a North American education, and enrolled for the *American School's* correspondence courses.

I quickly discovered that the material I had to study was much below the level of my earlier education in Germany. So I promptly terminated the course with the intention of getting into evening classes at a College instead. I eventually did this in Montreal, where, over a four-year period at considerable expenditure in time and effort and also—in relative terms, compared to my income at the time—in money, I obtained my first Canadian University degree.

My employment with this firm at their Winnipeg branch and—following a transfer at my request—in Montreal continued over twelve years. I gradually progressed into a series of managerial responsibilities. I even survived in my career and continued to thrive professionally following our take-over by another firm that had previously been a major competitor. By the time I left for totally different assignments in Ontario—to start a new career, indeed, a new life—the last position I held was that of Assistant General Manager of a major division.

I hesitate to describe my experiences in my country of choice during those early years as "A Canadian Success Story". But never once since my arrival did I regret my decision to emigrate from Germany, lament my lot, or deplore the difference in local customs from those to which I had previously been accustomed. I tried to fit in as best I could and become Canadian. Not only in citizenship on the first possible date, but more importantly in outlook and conduct and lifestyle. It seems to have worked for me!

GREENHORN IN CANADA

My fellow-immigrants and I, as newcomers in the early fifties, really did some peculiar things. I do not recall if, at the time of these missteps, I ever became embarrassed when I recognized my blunders.

After only a few days in Canada, I became aware that winter starts early in Manitoba and that you had to be equipped with overshoes. I bought mine in a tiny junky-looking store on Winnipeg's Main Street, paying the exact price asked. Later in the day I was told that I had no doubt disappointed the shop-keeper, who surely expected me to haggle for a lower price. I found this con-firmed when, on the following day, I accompanied another recent immigrant to the same store to buy an identical pair. After a lively negotiation, the cost was reduced by almost half of what I had previously paid. This was my first lesson as an astute shopper in my new country.

One of my shipmates had met a "very influential" resident of our chosen country Canada, during this chap's previous visit to his birthplace in Germany. Once we located him he turned out to be a driver for one of the minor taxi firms in the city. Another lesson learned was that not every alleged "rich uncle from Amerika"—in this case Kanada—is as wealthy as he would lead you to believe when he visits his "old country".

One of my early bosses, the manager of the branch office where I worked at the time, always expressed himself in a rather colourful way. His salty expletives added much to my vocabulary. In my ignorance I assumed that, if I ever wanted to become a manager in Canada, I had to expand my own vernacular in this dimension. It took me a while to learn otherwise, and then re-sanitize my lingo.

Following some "expert advice" before I came to Canada, I had acquired an International Driver's License in addition to my German Führerschein. Now I discovered that this had been an unnecessary expense. I still required a valid license for Manitoba, which entailed a written examination and an actual road test. Part of this was to parallel-park, where you *backed into* a parking space between two vehicles stationed at the curb, something I had never practiced nor even heard about. I failed in my first attempt and was directed to reappear in thirty days, after I had gained some experience in this, for me, novel routine. I had no difficulties during my second driving examination.

My first car was meant as a transport for four people; or five at the most. Yet I occasionally carried as many as seven passengers. On trips with this newly acquired light-green *1939 Willy's Overland* into the countryside around Winnipeg, my friends and I were constantly searching for forests, but always in vain. Whenever we approached an apparently wooded area that had appeared on the horizon, it revealed itself as just another "private property", at times merely a few trees planted around a farmer's house. We conscientiously stayed outside of all fenced-in areas, no matter how attractive they appeared. Eventually one of my colleagues revealed to me that, in Canada, barriers were erected to keep cattle *in*, not to keep people *out*.

My friends and I shared a common ignorance of the golf game. During one of our visits to an assumed public park, we observed a golfer who played in our direction. His warning cry of "fore" provoked no reaction from us. But surely, we thought, he would need his missile returned to undertake another shot. We obliged him by throwing the golf ball towards him. After our second such exertion he packed up his equipment and, accompanied by his, without a doubt, equally mystified caddy in tow, moved along to the next hole.

For our first Canadian vacation we drove to Alberta. While tenting in the wilderness near Banff, we eventually learned from a Forest Ranger that we should have obtained a fire permit. He had spent much of a morning searching for the source of smoke, which was detected by one of their observation towers. We had created this while we cooked our coffee and fried our breakfast bacon and eggs on an open fire. The general concern was, of course, about forest fires, which were—and still are today—a real threat in much of the outdoors.

After the move to Montreal in 1954, my initial week there exposed me to a novel way of traffic law enforcement—or rather to the lack of it. My car battery was dead, but payday was not for another week. It would never have occurred to me to withdraw any of my meagre savings from the bank, or—worse still—to buy something on credit. I therefore parked the car—by then I had upgraded to a black *1947 Mercury*—for the entire week in a "thirty minute" zone. And I did not get even one ticket for parking illegally.

Driving in general was quite different as well. At that time, throughout Quebec, neither pedestrians nor drivers seemed to pay much attention to the rules of the road. Traffic lights and stop signs appeared to serve as decoration rather than for control. It did not take me long to adjust my driving habits and deteriorate to the local level.

New to Montreal, my soon-to-be wife was not discouraged by the "bilingual" requirement listed in a Help-Wanted advertisement. She went there anyway, confidently stating that, with her knowledge of English and German, she did indeed have this talent. That's not what the company had in mind, of course, but they hired her anyway.

In our total innocence, we did not realize that a *kosher* butcher's shop was not the place to buy pork chops. We were somewhat bewildered when the owner directed us to his *goyim* competitors across the street.

In December 1955 we purchased our first ever brand-new automobile. It was the 1956 model of the *Ford Meteor Niagara*; with Colonial-white and Bermuda-blue as the two-tone colors. Since we did not want to expose this new vehicle to the harsh Montreal winter, our instructions to *Robitaille Motors* on Decarie Boulevard were to delay delivery until April. When the dealer called us early in January to advise that our new car had arrived, we reminded him of the later delivery initially requested.

As we were working during the day, we claimed the car after dark on the intended date early in April. It was, therefore, not until daylight the following morning when we discovered our pride-and-joy to be filthy inside, and also noticed that the speedometer and odometer did not function. A return trip to *Robitaille* resolved all visible problems.

It was some time thereafter when we finally realized the obvious cause for the earlier predicament. These people had been driving our new car, for who knows how many miles and under what conditions, with the odometer disconnected. At that time we were not aware of any law against such shenanigans by a dealer. But we felt some satisfaction the year after, when we learned that this firm had gone out of business.

Our current crop of immigrants will surely have their own perplexing experiences, just like my friends and I did at the time of our arrival. If these newcomers live here long enough they, too, will learn, just like others did before them. And eventually, when they trawl the depths of their recollections about these puzzling occurrences during their pioneering days, I would hope that they will be just as amused as I can now be about my own.

LEARNING ENGLISH

At the age of ten I had my first exposure to English. Until then, as my speaking language, I used my "high German" during school classes or when addressing strangers; and *Brigandedeutsch,* the local dialect of Karlsruhe, with family and friends, even with some teachers during recess. It seemed generally recognized that, while in Northern Germany communication in regionalized parlance demonstrated the speaker's limited education, in the South, where I grew up, it was considered a display of local pride—indeed, of *anti-Prussian-ness.*

Along with English as my first foreign language, I was also taught Latin, a few years thereafter French and—much later still—Spanish as well. Throughout my life, while travelling extensively on business and for pleasure, I was to learn some fifteen words or more in the many different *lingoes* of the foreign countries I visited.

During my early school years, instruction in Latin was a wasted effort, and my report cards reflected this. The unlikely event of ever encountering an ancient Roman, with whom I could chat in Latin, might explain my lack of enthusiasm. I also had no plans to either become a doctor or join the priesthood, with both professions requiring the knowledge of Latin.

Even in English, which—at the beginning of World War Two—might have equipped us, the future soldiers of the *Reich,* for the anticipated imminent occupation of Britain, the instructions were dull/dull/dull. Emphasis seemed to be on grammar; and whatever stories we learned to recite were ancient tales without any practical application. Therefore, I found even the English lessons rather boring, and—as a result—did not distinguish myself with linguistic accomplishments.

My first ever practical application of English was during April 1945, when—after more than four years of tutoring—I really had to struggle to convey my intentions to one of our occupiers. This French soldier, claiming to speak English, appeared even less fluent than I.

An exchange of territory among the Allies made my hometown part of the U.S. Zone of Occupation. From then on I took every opportunity to chat with the *Amis,* the members of the American forces. Frequent interchanges were necessary because of my active pursuit of the many beneficial opportunities offered in the black market.

To illustrate my initially somewhat challenging efforts, I must explain that the German words for *buy* and *sell* were *kaufen* and *verkaufen*. The English term "sell" was unknown to me, when I tried to convey its meaning during one of my transactions. Using the logic of the German words, I indicated that "I want to buy this *to* you". As I simultaneously showed my merchandise, and accompanied my uttering with lots of *Körpersprache* (body English), the American G.I. understood and traded my wares—a silver ring and some home-brew liquor—for the cigarettes and chocolate bars that I desired.

Hit Kits were the sheet music that I scrounged and collected whenever possible. They presented the text along with the notes of the *American Hit Parade* songs, to which I listened continuously on *AFN* (the American Forces Network). Learning them by heart—to the occasional dismay of my grandchildren I can still recite many of them today—greatly increased my vocabulary.

From my American "business contacts" I was able to collect a fair number of paperbacks, most of them Westerns and other "low-brow" literature. Through attentive reading, I enhanced my word power as well.

Pen-pals in foreign countries were all the rage in post-war Germany. In amateurish English I corresponded with Japan, the U.S.A., and—above all—with England. This, too, allowed me to practice and thereby improve my linguistic skills.

With one of my friends, a classmate, it was arranged for each of us to introduce a new English word when we met in school every day. One of those he provided was "Timber", also used as the warning cry of foresters. This might have been a portent of my much later designation as a lumberjack for my Canadian immigration.

My English teacher at that time, very much with the old-fashioned tutoring, knew everything about grammar. But slang—the mere term as such—was something totally unknown to him. When I asked what "*Gonna*" meant in the then popular hit "*Gonna take a sentimental journey*", he suggested that it might be someone's name.

After four years of *practical* application, I considered myself slightly fluent in the English language, certainly way above the level required for my graduation exams. My pronunciation—if you could overlook the German accent—had considerable inflections of the American variety. This resulted in my final marks for the *Abitur* (senior matriculation) being down-graded by one level. During the oral examination, the then English teacher—he was never my favourite, nor was I his—corrected my American intonation. So much for trying to get the best mark in English!

In my working environment once in Canada, I became familiar with many English expressions, for which the proper German would have been a new experience as well. Whenever I had to convey these descriptions in my first language, I improvised as best I could. "Ocean Bill of Lading" was one of these minor challenges. Since a "Bill of Lading" was a *Frachtbrief* in German, I assumed that I could use "*Ozean Frachtbrief*" in my German communications. I later discovered that the proper description should have been *Konnossement*.

On other occasions I struggled for the German word, simply to discover that, as part of the *Americanization of Europe*, the English depiction was the only one applied. "Publicity" was one of these.

While I still lived in Montreal, following some extensive psychological testing for a potential multinational employer, I was able to obtain a copy of the Placement Agency's report to their client. It was astounding for me to discover their assessment of my capabilities in what was my second language. With a verbal aptitude in English of above 93% of those *college*-educated in North America; they also ranked me above 97 out of 100 persons in logic, critical thinking and conclusion reaching within the same group.

At that time, someone could still have impressed me with an array of academic degrees. It was some years later when, involved with the recruiting and employment of professionals with English as their native tongue and more advanced university standing than my own, that I became disillusioned. The very basics of learning, such as grammar and spelling, or arithmetic, did not seem to be prerequisites for some schools of higher learning.

Since then, either our Canadian educational system has improved immensely, or that of other countries greatly deteriorated. Otherwise, how can one explain the well-publicised recent PISA study (Program for International Student Assessment), which lists our Canadian accomplishments as #3 out of thirty-two countries, while Germany is at best an "also ran", with a ranking in the mid-twenties. Whatever happened to their schooling, as I had experienced it as a youngster? And how could ours in Canada have advanced so much, totally unnoticed by me?

EXPLORING MY COUNTRY

My wife Gussie and I enjoyed extensive travel in all ten Canadian Provinces. Yet—after more than fifty years—the Territories in the north are still awaiting our first visit; including Nunavut, which reached the status of a separate jurisdiction as recent as April of 1999.

After we became parents, our son Kenneth also accompanied us during repeat visits to Alberta and British Columbia. And, of course, as a family, the three of us lived together in Quebec and in Ontario. Much more recently I now explore Canada from coast to coast with my grandchildren.

The very early trips from our first residence in Winnipeg, and later from Montreal, we usually did "on the cheap". The transport was always our automobile. A few times we brought a tent for camping. On a couple of occasions the car served as our sleeping quarter. Security, in those days, was not a concern. Danger might only rarely come from marauding bears or other wildlife, but never from humans.

During these initial explorations, when we sought accommodation, it was in a motel with a reasonable rate. Once or twice we selected what later would become known as "bed and breakfast" places.

The food that we brought from home would nourish us during the first day of travel. Thereafter, we always took our main meal in the evening. Breakfast, except on the rare occasion when, while camping, we cooked it on an open fire, would be of the elaborate North American variety. Lunch was a snack, accompanied by much fruit, which was also what we *noshed* on throughout the day.

Gasoline was inexpensive; yet, in Canada, never quite as amazingly cheap as the lowest ever, at 16 (sixteen!) US cents *per gallon*. This we experienced but once, during a price war of competing gasoline stations at a highway intersection somewhere in New Jersey. There were four quarts (equalling not quite four litres, if you no longer recall this peculiar type of measurement), in one US gallon. The imperial gallon, then still used in Canada, had about 4½ of the US quarts each.

When we travelled to distant places, we started before daybreak. At time for a late breakfast we had already covered 200 miles. Our normal daily mileage reached 500. Converted into the metric system, this was 800 kilometres for the day.

While we lived in Manitoba, we did much evening and weekend exploring throughout the Province. A northern venture to Churchill I undertook on my own—this was early in 1952—during my brief career as a second cook with *CN* railways.

From the base in Winnipeg, our vacations brought us to Western Canada. We quickly passed through Saskatchewan's wheat fields. Half a day in Regina and the same on the return through Saskatoon covered it all, we thought. From my *big-city-slicker* perspective, I was able to confirm our earlier assessment during a number of business trips some years later. But beyond the Prairies lay "the Promised Land" of Alberta and British Columbia. Gussie and I visited these two beautiful Provinces on several occasions; and again many years later, when we were accompanied by our son. By then we had, of course, long progressed to air travel, rental cars, good hotels, and fancy restaurants.

In our "pioneering" days, we never judged our quality-of-life experiences by the economic stratum at which we could afford to travel. It was instead very much the breathtaking environment that we viewed, the wildlife we observed, and the unspoiled nature at its very best that surrounded us.

On our first visit to Victoria, the capital of British Columbia, Gussie and I had our picture taken at the sign (showing miles, of course), which indicated the end of the Trans-Canada Highway. Many years later, during the summer of 1998, we viewed the marker at point 0.0 (by now recorded in kilometres) of this 7,604 km road in St. John's, Newfoundland's capital city, where it begins.

Before the direct Trans-Canada Highway connection was established through Rogers Pass between Revelstoke and Golden in 1962, it was necessary to drive an extended detour on the original Big Bend Highway. Gussie and I were on our way from British Columbia to Alberta and had expected to take the longer route the following morning. We spent the night in Revelstoke, without much sleep. Our street-side accommodation did not shield us from the incessant car honking that went on throughout the night.

As we discovered the next day, the *Loyal Order of Moose* (or was it the *Benevolent and Protective Order of Elks?*) had held a Convention, which, in transit, brought their membership to this small community. Those who could not get or did not want to rent a hotel room drove around most of the night and, whenever they encountered another Moose or Elk (either name quite appropriate for their membership, no doubt), they honked their car horns at each other.

But this gathering of *large furry animals* was also a blessing in disguise, as an escorted drive over the not yet completed—but nevertheless somehow passable—new stretch of the Trans-Canada Highway had been arranged for them.

We followed along and saved several hours in transit. Today the original Big Bend Highway is partially under water because of the flooding of the valley, when two dams were built.

On a visit to Jasper National Park, while the rest of the family slept late one morning, I went for a long walk. On my return to our hotel I encountered several bears picking berries among the foliage ahead of me. I tried to follow the experts' advice to avoid them by backing away. But not for very long, since they were blocking the only path towards our hotel. I therefore clapped my hands and started singing softly. It was either my off-key singing, my clapping, or the knocking sound of my knees that made the beasts disappear into the more distant forest.

Back at the hotel, both my wife and my son found my tale hard to believe—until later that day, when we encountered more bears, and my reputation as a factual raconteur was re-established.

A visit to EXPO 86 in Vancouver I did on my own, in conjunction with a business trip during which I was able to view this international exhibition. What I recall most vividly is the Closing Ceremony on October 13th 1986. For the march of the exhibiting nations into the stadium, the participants from the U.S.A. and of the U.S.S.R. joined into one happy group. You must remember that, in those days, many Americans still considered the Soviet Union to be "the evil empire". Witnessing the demonstration of togetherness and unity among these youngsters brought tears to my eyes.

From the time of our much earlier move to Quebec in 1954, we spent many a weekend in the beautiful Laurentians, the cottage and vacation area north of Montreal. Yet what I remember from there, more than anything else, were the swarms of mosquitoes which seemed to pester us continually, just as shad flies did along the St. Lawrence River in the spring, when we spent any time there.

The Maritimes, the destination for one of our vacations out of Montreal, proved to be another attractive part of our country. During frequent business trips and further family holidays, I was to view its sights on many more occasions in later years.

From our first visit there, I recall one night's accommodation in New Brunswick that was a bit unusual. It was very late in the evening and extremely foggy, when we selected what turned out to be a "room for rent" private residence for our night's stay. The lady who received us was a rather gloomy-looking person, who told us something about her son having died recently. His name sounded Scandinavian, we thought it was Olaf. During the night we heard these haunting calls "Ooooolaaaaaf" and again "Ooooolaaaaaf", over and over again. Spooky, we thought, as we huddled closer together. In the morning we realized that these supposed human cries of agony emanated from foghorns, directing the fishermen who were still on the ocean.

Until we became Canadian citizens, a visa to enter the U.S.A. would have been required. We still didn't have one but, as an experiment, drove up to the U.S. border station in Alberta's Waterton Lakes National Park. The question "Where were you born" (still legal at that time) I answered truthfully with "Karlsruhe". "Is that in Manitoba" was the next query, as our car had Manitoba license plates. Since I insisted on telling the truth, we were barred from entry into Montana's Waterton Glacier International Peace Park for lack of the proper visa.

Halfway between the U.S. and the Canadian border checkpoints, our car engine stalled. With much commotion and cheerful volunteer help from immigration officials on both sides of the border, the *'47 Mercury* eventually started again, enabling us to continue our journey on the Canadian side of "the longest undefended border in the world".

It was a year or two later when, for the very first time, we would be authorized to travel to the United States.

THE U.S. OF A.

On April 9th 1955, at Champlain in New York State, my wife and I entered the United States of America for the very first time. In our German passports we had finally obtained a visa, then still provided free of charge, allowing unlimited entry into our neighbouring country.

With only two exceptions, Gussie and I, together, experienced every single one of the States of the USA, over the years before our son was born. Thereafter, Kenneth as well accompanied us frequently to New York; to all the States in New England, most often Maine; and for a couple of visits to Florida.

As did most Montreal residents in those days, we made frequent trips across the border to shop in close-by Plattsburg/New York or Burlington/Vermont, at much reduced prices. On returning from one of these trips "abroad", my *1947 Mercury* malfunctioned right in the middle of a multi-track railway crossing in LaPrairie, Quebec. Once outside the automobile, we could hear an approaching train. Brute force pushed our only means of transport to a more appropriate spot. And my comment in *Franglish* of "*Mon muffler est détoné*" to a local French-speaking mechanic brought prompt assistance, which eventually allowed us to continue our travel home.

On another occasion, we visited New York City. Not a bad hotel at all where we stayed, but it offered no inside garage space to accommodate our car. Once we parked in the street, a police officer quickly cautioned us to leave nothing of value inside. He also advised to keep the car doors unlocked, to avoid the windshields being smashed by investigating rogues.

Right after the purchase of our *1956 Meteor*, we decided to equip it with seat covers. This was the general practice at the time. Perhaps one wanted to keep the original upholstery clean for an eventual resale? Whatever the reason, acquiring the covers in the States was much cheaper. We bought ours in Plattsburg and had to install them there, to avoid questioning by Canadian border officials and the possible customs duties, when we returned home. As the owner and driver of the car, I was elected to do the installation in a public parking lot, while my passengers went to do more shopping.

With our still almost brand-new *Meteor*, my wife and I drove to California. Between Salt Lake City/Utah and Reno/Nevada, there was one stretch of road through the desert, well identified as such to caution travellers, which provided no habitation or service outlet for exactly 50 miles. Right at the halfway point of this desolate area, our vehicle ceased to run. At that time one could still do the odd repair oneself. Despite my lack of engineering talent, even I had been changing oil and filter and spark plugs and points on my cars for years. But in this case, none of the technical knowledge that I possessed helped in our predicament.

Eventually my spouse hitched a ride with one of the rarely passing motorists, to search for a technician some 25 miles ahead. I remained behind, still trying to get a sound out of the silent starter. To no avail, until the mechanic arrived. He leaned under the hood and asked me to push the starter button. And what do you know; *vroom-vroom* and we were back in business. It cost us 25 American dollars for the service call.

The car worked fine for the rest of the trip. But a couple of months later, in downtown Montreal during rush hour, the same problem occurred. This time the vehicle was towed to my local mechanic, a guy who really knew his stuff. Even he had to experiment at great length, to finally discover the cause of the problem. Much later the manufacturer sent a notice to service outlets, identifying the problem that had occurred on many vehicles of this particular model.

Being stopped for speeding in the United States was an interesting experience. On a Thruway in New York State we were pulled over. The officer took my drivers license and the keys. We had to wait while more cars were apprehended for the same offence. Then the entire convoy was instructed to follow the officer, who still held onto everyone's papers. In a small town we appeared before a Justice of the Peace, who arrived in shirtsleeves while still chewing on a sandwich. I pleaded "guilty" to the charges against me, paid the fine in cash, and proceeded on the way home to Montreal.

The children's rhyme of the "Inzy Winzy Spider" is something Gussie and I will never forget. It was what his mother read for our son while she held Kenneth in her arms on our way to Wells Beach/Maine, where we usually spent a week or two during the summer. "One more time, Mommy" he must have said a hundred times. And his Mommy did oblige!

That was before airbags, baby seats or safety belts as equipment in automobiles. The usual practice was for parents to have their small children in the front seat of the car, mostly on someone's lap. The danger of this routine never occurred to anyone.

Hawaii and Alaska were the only States that I had to visit on my own, in conjunction with business trips into Asia. The closest I came to a grizzly bear in Alaska was while standing next to the big fellow they have stuffed and exhibited inside the airport in Anchorage.

When during a *luau* in Hawaii they served the usual roasted pig and the traditional *poi,* I found the meat extremely salty and—not that I had ever ingested wallpaper glue before—suspected that *poi* had such a taste. Only for my second such meal during another lay-over did I learn that pork, when dipped in *poi,* made both components taste much better.

Geographical segments like this, where I covered the rest of my frequently travelled world in an earlier volume, could all have been expanded. Yet, including descriptions—from a tourist's perspective—of the many wonderful places I viewed, was never intended for my written recollections. The entire series of trekking journals was to be an anecdotal autobiography and not a travelogue. Therefore, I tried throughout to curtail my usual youthful exuberance, even if my discoveries would have been worthy of any sightseer's adoration.

TRAVEL SINCE 9/11

With the destruction of New York's World Trade Center on September 11th 2001, our *total war* with terrorism finally became a priority. One result was that security procedures for travellers at most airports significantly increased. Whether they actually "improved" is another question.

I was able to voice my opinion about this at the airport in Frankfurt, when I was interviewed—in German—by one of their television stations. After just having undergone a particularly thorough examination, I indicated that, while I understood why authorities had *to be seen* to be doing something, I did not expect this to keep "the bad guys" from committing their nasty deeds. To their further question I declared that I did *not* feel any safer after having gone through their elaborate *Sicherheitskontrolle*, nor that I ever worried about such things in the first place. The day following my return, my cousin telephoned to advise that she had viewed me giving my commentary during two successive newscasts on the *Deutsche Welle*.

Accusations of "racial profiling"—an approach which, to me, makes a great deal of sense—must create concern for the authorities and apprehension among the personnel performing the security examinations. For reasons of "political correctness" they can not make their real selection criteria too obvious. As a result, so I suspect, they have to occasionally identify the most unlikely travellers for a thorough search and evaluation. A 10-year old ethnic Chinese boy; an 80-year old black grandmother; or a *very* Danish-looking young woman, such as my daughter-in-law; would all conform in their look of innocence to become a sacrificial lamb.

It was Birte who experienced this during a recent transfer at Heathrow Airport. For further interrogation and closer scrutiny of all their paraphernalia, the security staff selected several of their Arab-looking youngish male passengers—since it is the brethren of these who provide many of today's terrorists. They also chose the mother of my grandchildren as their only token victim who, most visibly, did not match the generally anticipated appearance of a suspected suicidal mass-murderer.

Stricter enforcement of regulations and more thorough examinations—all resulting in lengthier processing at the transportation terminals—do not upset me. I still enjoy travelling immensely. But only to the destinations which fit my current interests. Florida with my spouse in the winter; Europe during the summer; and somewhere in Canada—anywhere that they like to go—with my grandchildren during the school holidays.

There is only one thing that, as a traveller, I really miss since my retirement. It is the seating and service in the airlines' Business Class. While my employers paid for it, I was able to enjoy this perk. It was a good investment for the organization since, whatever the time difference at my destination even after a lengthy flight, I always commenced working at their local hours promptly after arrival.

Gussie and I now regularly travel with "the great unwashed". To have the additional conveniences, the increase in the airfare is just too much for us to take from the kids' inheritance. But, despite our seating in Economy, I usually end up with the right kind of newspaper by merely asking for it early enough. I also rarely miss out on my after-dinner *Drambuie*—actually two of them with my refills of tea—as probably the only passenger being so served in my section of the aircraft.

To be a happy traveller, one just has to know how to ask. And, of course, it also helps to be blessed with my charming personality, eh?

MY FELLOW CANUCKS

Most of my readers will not be old enough to have encountered *Johnny Canuck*, supposedly *reintroduced* as the label for our countrymen with a cartoon character during World War Two. Perhaps it is just an urban legend that the initial inception goes back to 1867, the year of our Confederation, with the hero being launched as a political caricature, depicting a younger cousin of the Yank's *Uncle Sam* and the Brit's *John Bull.*

My first-ever direct contact with a Canadian was during the interview before my immigration visa could be issued. Judging by his name and appearance, the interrogating officer appeared to be a *WASP*. I distinctly recall his RAF-type moustache. His ruddy complexion made me suspect his frequent consumption of alcohol.

He was the one who classified me as a *lumberjack* and still directed me to Regina. Since they grow wheat and not trees in Saskatchewan, he couldn't have been very knowledgeable about Canada, so I surmised much later.

In recent years there was a supposedly funny and quite popular program on television; I do not recall the network that presented this. It poked gentle fun at our southern neighbours, because of their alleged ignorance of things Canadian. The format was interviews with well-known or at least "well-educated" Americans.

During the American election campaign, they even caught *George W.* The then candidate for the presidency of the United States thanked them sincerely for the good wishes that they professed to convey from our Prime Minister *Jean Poutine.* "*Poutine*" is, of course, a popular fast-food item in the Province of Quebec, something that Jean Chrétien himself—just like I—might enjoy occasionally. Not generally considered a great intellect, at least not by the insolent media of our time, Bush might well have mistaken the name for "Putin", the head honcho of another big country.

How can we expect others to be knowledgeable about Canada, especially the culturally self-absorbed Americans, when our own compatriots are not that well-informed either? Unless they live in the immediate area, how many of our citizens pronounce the name of the most easterly Province correctly as Newfound*land,* with emphasis on the last syllable? And who, outside of British Columbia, knows that Victoria, their Capital City, is on Vancouver Island, while Vancouver, the metropolis, lies on the mainland? Can we all identify the capitals of Alberta, New Brunswick, or even Ontario? And who names more than one or two of our Provincial Premiers, or—most certainly with this example—who cares? For others than those governing Alberta, Ontario or Quebec—and, because of a slight similarity in family names, Gary *Doer* from Manitoba—even I might have to consult the *internet*.

Are Canadians aware that the *Trans-Canada*, at just under 8000 kilometres, is the longest highway, or that, at almost 1200 km, Toronto's *Yonge Street* is the world's longest street? Can we name our doctors Banting and Best as the discoverers of *Insulin*? But, why would anyone want to know that it was a chap from Toronto, who invented the *Paint Roller*. It's *aficionados* of such minutiae, who made the *Trivial Pursuit* board game, also conceived by two of our compatriots, such a success.

Even if unable to recite historical and geographical minutiae, or our major achievements—be they ridiculous or sublime—what, in unison, all Canadians can state categorically, is that we are *not* Americans. Which, of course, is incorrect, since—while neither Yankees nor from Dixie—we are certainly North Americans, just like they are. But then, so are the Mexicans. Yet I doubt if they would be as preoccupied, as we are as Canadians, with emphasizing that they are *not* from the U.S. of A.

Most of our residents seem to be much more familiar with the culture, geography and the history of their ancestral lands, than with their chosen country Canada. Is it because their *dinosaur* nations, with an immensely longer history, have so many more ancient events to shout about? In comparison, with the recording of our traditions and historical facts, we appear much like *teenagers* with our relatively youthful existence.

Perhaps it is also the multicultural mumbo-jumbo promoted by federal and provincial jurisdictions, which makes us more knowledgeable about our roots abroad. Such levels of ethnic preoccupation often continue even with the Canadian-born descendants.

Just one recent occurrence can illustrate this point. It was during the week leading up to *Canada Day*, when my son displayed our Canadian flag in his front window. The international soccer championships were still being played at that time. A neighbour, originally from one of the participating countries, questioned Kenneth about this, since, so he observed, Canada wasn't even competing in the games.

Historically, there has always been the debate—albeit, in global terms, not much of a "struggle"—between the Anglo and Franco elements in our society. Yet both these groups were part of "the Western world".

In recent years, a new and, no doubt, ever-lasting predicament has been introduced to Canada—indeed to the U.S.A. and many European countries as well. Over the centuries, mainstream Canadians had always been part of a Judaic-Christian culture and civilization. Arrivals from other environments were relatively small in number and eventually adjusted and merged into the majority. As I see it, this is no more.

Overwhelming numbers of our current immigrants come from the Third World, at times far removed in customs, mores and values from what we consider *our* civilization. Those from Latin America, from the Philippines and from Central and Southern Africa, because of their either Christian or other—minute in Canadian numbers—fractious cultural backgrounds, should eventually mesh seamlessly into the predominating establishment. Not as easily some of those from Muslim countries.

With the benevolent understanding or, perhaps, even acute embarrassment of their own more sophisticated former countrymen, who also make Canada their new home, a few of these recent arrivals may never *want to* "fit". At least in their own minds and with the indoctrination of their young children, they struggle to continue living within a still enduring medieval social structure from their places of origin to which, as members of a social "underclass", they always belonged. Hopefully the new milieu will eventually convert their offspring to a 21st century environment—very much against the wishes of their elders, of course.

The talking heads on television and other media types comment passionately about our immigration policy—mostly about the apparent *lack* of one. A few even dare to deplore the import of so many of "the great unwashed", who come without the allegedly necessary qualifications to integrate as Canadians.

Yet this is not the problem, as I see it. Being illiterate does not mean being ignorant. Such people from around the world acquire their training and wisdom with daily experiences in "the book of life". Our country was built by many of these "un-educated", with at least their offspring adjusting fully and becoming successful.

Our long-term challenge, so I believe, evolves only from those among the huge number of recent immigrants, who refuse to integrate, adapt, or even accommodate the views of those previously established in our country. Although most of our current arrivals, wherever they are from, just try to make a better life for themselves and their families, as the majority of settlers did over generations.

I do recall the time when everyone with a German name or accent was considered a Nazi or at least a sympathizer. That is why I particularly abhor the thought that anyone with a brown skin, an Arab name, or Islam as the religion, could be branded a radical; generalizing a Western perception of what is merely a minute part of this group. However, the absence of any real condemnation of the fanatical extremists' aims and actions, by our Muslim countrymen in general, concerns me greatly.

Because of the evil intentions or deeds of a tiny minority, their cultural group in its entirety could well be judged a growing force of "them" opposed to "us". Canada's future *Two Solitudes* may, indeed, be the combatants who have been struggling on and off for some fifteen hundred years. The *Crusades* and the *Jihad* will have found a—hopefully, albeit, much more civilized and somewhat subdued—battleground in our country.

THE FRENCH FACT

Throughout our stay in Montreal during the 1950s and the early 1960s, I had little opportunity to practice my French. At that time, the workers seemed to be exclusively French speaking. In factories or businesses such as ours, the foremen spoke French "down" to the workforce and English "up" to their management. The executives of many larger firms were primarily *Anglos* or, as *les autres* from diverse ethnic backgrounds, generally not conversant in French. The language of business was English for sure.

As I was part of management, whenever I addressed any of my staff in French, they responded in English. Perhaps just as well, since most of our employees usually spoke *patois*, the local dialect, which I might not have understood. In hindsight, I recognized much later that I should have made more of an effort. I could, in fact, have let it be known that I preferred to practice my French, rather than be humoured with a response in English. I might even have acquired some fluency in Quebec's regional *lingo*. And I could certainly have conversed effectively with all those of my contacts who spoke a more sophisticated French.

But then, why should I have made the effort? Wasn't it the task of the "natives" to accommodate the members of the "ruling class"—albeit in my case at an insignificantly low rank? With such an attitude that, to my amazement, I found to be prevalent among at least some of the non-*Francophone* of that time, it was perhaps not surprising that, towards the end of our stay in Montreal, separatism in Quebec became a serious threat for the unilingual *Anglos*.

Jean Lesage, the Liberal Premier of *la belle province* from 1960 to 1966, had introduced the slogan *Maîtres chez-nous*—Masters in our home—with his 1962 election campaign. It was in his government that René Lévesque served as a cabinet minister until, as leader of the *Parti Québécois* in 1976, he himself became Premier, the first ever under the separatist banner.

Lévesque—a man I really admired—had all my sympathies, when he officially converted to separatism in 1967. I did not feel then, nor dare I hope now, that the French fact in Canada will be able to survive as part of the united country in its present form. And, of course, the bicultural English-French commotion evolves and continues despite our often enthusiastic and always costly efforts for a nation-wide development of bilingualism.

A complicating factor may well be the mishmash of a growing multitude of government-supported ethnic organizations, reflecting the much propagated and—from my perspective—at times divisive multicultural societies; something I very much deplore.

My aspirations for Canada have always been to retain it as a bilingual and bicultural country. This was to be English and French exclusively, with everything else considered "alien". I could accept the ambitions of some French-Canadians to be called "a nation"; just as long as the Anglo component of our country is recognized as "a nation" as well. Arrivals from other cultures—with me very much included—would then have to decide on their "*Canadian* nation of choice", or remain as foreigners forever. I recognize constantly that I have made the right selection!

Considering today's regrettable *multi-culti* reality, for the French identity to remain in a meaningful way, it might—in the opinion of nationalists—indeed become necessary for *Québécois* to establish a unilingual country of their own. Of course, this may not be a cost-effective way of living, but merely one for ethnic, cultural, and linguistic survival. Although, in today's global community, this could well remain an impossible dream. Yet isn't Canada, my chosen country, an example of heart and soul over mind and money? Perhaps, exclusively for economic reasons, some of us, too, might be better off as part of a larger North America. But I for one would never want to trade the privilege of living in Canada for the possible mere financial advantage of our being part of the United States.

Despite my sympathies for the Canadian French in their struggle for survival on an English-speaking continent—indeed in a more and more English-speaking world—I have my personal prejudices to accommodate and my own feelings to live with. And I must state categorically that anyone trying to break up my country—for whatever lofty reason—is no friend of mine.

It was French President Charles de Gaulle, during a speech from a balcony of the Montreal City Hall in 1967, who rallied the nationalists with his cry of "*Vive le Québec libre*". Some of his cohorts, so I suspect, had always been stirring the separatist caldron of political intrigue and unrest in our Province of Quebec, with their clandestine support for a "New France".

My personal reaction was an immediate ban on French products. My job, however, took me to France several times each year. While this necessitated a hotel room, local transportation and meals during my many stays, I refused to purchase anything of a personal nature. Had I run out of toothpaste, for example, I would have done without it until I reached the next country on my itinerary. Quite petty? Certainly! Totally useless? Of course! But, while I recognized it as a patently absurd endeavour, for me this was a matter of principle!

I had the same reaction to the Province of Quebec, as long as their separatist government was in power. I even refused to venture there, no matter how much I would have liked to visit. Strangely enough, since I merely lived there for twelve years of my life, I always considered Montreal to be "my" home town.

Our son was born in Montreal. When separation became a frightening possibility a few years after our 1966 move to Toronto, he expressed his concern. "Will I still be a Canadian, when they separate?" was his worry. I convincingly reassured him; and can sincerely express my passionate wish for all *Québécois* to remain as Canadians forever.

NOBLE SAVAGES

The Indians lost the competition, although in Canada not in actual warfare. They were equally gypped out of their land on both sides of the 49th parallel. But—perhaps that's where both our governments run by former Europeans really messed up—they were never absorbed, integrated, forced into the general population of their, by sheer numbers, overpowering vanquishers.

In the early days, so we are told, many of their forebears were decimated by TB, smallpox, VD, or otherwise exterminated as the result of the European invasion. I am just being cynical, of course, when I occasionally state that the plight of today's Indians is really *my* responsibility. Since my race and culture matches that of the descendants of their alleged oppressors and historical exploiters, it is my fault and that of other *Euro-Canadians*. Our governments and the aborigine industry—their minority's administrators and lawyers—as well as many of our bleeding-heart elitists, profess this as the truth.

But who in this world hasn't suffered at one time or other, after being subdued by a more powerful invader. Some 90% (*ninety* percent) of my own ancestors perished, when their territory was ravaged by neighbouring forces from all over Europe during—to name but one of these ancient skirmishes—the Thirty-Years War. I realize that this was somewhat further back in history than the Indian confrontations.

Whom should I blame for these and the more recent sufferings of "my tribe" and pressure into paying *me* today, as the descendant of those so badly treated? Where to draw the line? To extend this into the preposterous, does one strive for compensation from the Allies of WW2? Although I recognize that their land-grabbing retaliatory action, no matter how ruthless, could well be discarded as merely a well-deserved punishment bestowed onto my former countrymen, who had been the initial aggressors. Somewhat more deservedly, could the Germans reproach the French because of the Napoleonic wars; the Turks of the Ottoman Empire; the Vikings; the ancient Romans; the hordes of the Slavic invaders? My unfortunate forebears, too, were overrun, beaten, dispossessed, enslaved, raped and killed. So were the residents of neighbouring countries, often by my own compatriots. Since none of us can qualify as a "deserving minority", we must consider all these atrocities as a closed issue—and I happily do so. *Might brought right*, and subjugation and exploitation had always been the practice.

When considering the dilemma with our Indians, we should allow that promises to the underdogs of a time, throughout the ages, were habitually made to be broken. Unlike, as but one example, during the negotiations with the railways in Canada, where these organizations' lawyers insisted on written contracts, our First Nations usually accepted the government representatives' spoken assurances, presented on behalf of "the Great White Mother (or Father)" of the time. Where the Indians ceded their territories in exchange for a pledge of perpetual consideration and care, they assumed to be dealing with honourable people. But even if the negotiators at that moment were sincere, generations of their successors dismissed the intent of the original agreements.

Only in recent years, with teams of lawyers of their own, do our First Nations take serious action to redress the earlier injustices. In theory, because I think of myself as a fair-minded person, I wish them well. Yet I am sufficiently pragmatic to deplore the continuing ruckus that they incite with their demonstrations, road blockades, and incessant whining. I am also quite apprehensive about the eventual cost of any settlements to me as a taxpayer.

Is it really the European influx that changed so many of these reportedly proud and self-sufficient "nations" into today's occasionally corrupt, lawless and deprived society? Are we responsible for their excessive suicide rate, alcoholism, gasoline-sniffing, incest, spousal abuse, lacking business acumen, and petty crime? If the Europeans had not arrived, would these historically self-reliant *almost*-Canadians still live in wigwams; hunt, fish and gather wild rice and berries for nourishment; traverse the country on foot or in canoes; and cure all their ailments in sweat lodges and with herbal remedies? I don't believe it!

I have great admiration for outstanding leaders such as the real-life Chief Geronimo of the Apaches. Yet for him, for his Indian brethren in the United States, and for ours here in Canada, their world had indeed come to an end. So why, over the few hundred years of their exposure to "Western civilization", didn't ours just make an effort to fit in with the rest of the community; merely endure and get it over with, and become Canadians?

But then, why should they? Through our growing obsession with official multiculturalism, a fair number of Canada's newest ethnic tribes, such as today's immigrants arriving from all over the world, strive not to do so either.

In the European history of my own ancestors, those Germans who settled in the area of the former Soviet Union, or in the Balkans, retained their separate and distinct traditions for a couple of centuries as well. And, of my most venerated people, the globally thriving Jews, many have effectively resisted integration and done so for millennia, while living among foreign and antagonistic civilizations. So how can I, without being a hypocrite, consider such a struggle for cultural survival an aberration, when it is done by our First Nations?

However, there is a major difference! In the history of these other groups, where they struggled to retain their distinctiveness in alien and often bellicose environments, they succeeded culturally and socially in remaining "above" their surroundings. They did not let themselves become absorbed into the mediocrity of their local fellows. As well, much unlike our natives, where these Jewish or German minorities were exposed to superior communities, they learned from these and accepted what they found useful, with adaptations for their own requirements. Pursuing the path taken by our Indians, today's Germans might still live in caves and wear bearskin clothes; and the Jews could well be forever wandering in the wilderness.

I cannot imagine a superior individual of the stature of Geronimo, or of our very own Shawnee Chief Tecumseh, blaming the "whiteys" for their lot, nor encouraging their followers to vegetate on hand-outs from their guilt-ridden former exploiters. Surely these outstanding personages would have moved with the times and adapted to the modern world. Either of them might have ended up as the head-honcho of a *BCE*, a *CBC* or a *CIBC* organization; Premier of a Province; or charismatic leader in another sphere of significance for the 21st century. In their case, it would certainly have been because of their very own talents, and not as the result of someone else's benevolent tokenism through affirmative action.

Where I grew up, the boys of my generation enjoyed Karl May as a favourite novelist. This German author wrote mainly about the Noble Savages in North America, and their struggle against a never-ending onslaught of whites, who viciously exploited the natives, stole their land and—with the chilling slogan "The only good Indian is a dead Indian"—pursued their objective to either starve or actually murder them *en masse*.

The literature's Indian Chief Winnetou and his compatriots were our idols. In the games we played as youngsters, the Indians were the heroes, while their white opponents were the bad guys.

Once in Canada, because of my childhood background so sympathetic to the Native Americans, I read some of the available literature; eagerly perused related media reports; and closely observed anything with an Indian affiliation, whenever I encountered it. I quickly became disillusioned and sorely disappointed.

The very first observation of my former heroes was through the drunk and dishevelled specimens that I encountered on the downtown streets of Winnipeg. Since that time I have not read about related current events nor personally seen anything that might have erased this unfortunate impression or improved on my earliest experience in Canada.

My—albeit extremely limited—personal contact with individual "First Nation" representatives has been equally disturbing. Those I encountered really exploited the system and capitalized on their Indian heritage.

There was a major organization's not even marginally qualified executive whose obvious talent seemed to be his contribution as the "token aborigine" to the firm's management team; a previously always ignored applicant to a police force, who was quickly recruited once his Indian ancestry could be documented—until then he had proudly professed to be a French Canadian; another one chuckling about the automobile he acquired without paying taxes, by listing his fake address on a reservation in Northern Ontario; and a fellow-shopper, who bragged about just acquiring a large supply of medications without any cost, while informing me that I was standing on "his" land—we were at the *Square One Shopping Centre* in Mississauga at the time. All seemed to be of mixed blood and—in a comparison of our original ancestry—my ethnic background might have turned out to be more Swiss or French, rather than German, than theirs was Indian.

During my fifty years as a Canadian, I must indeed have encountered a fair number of responsible citizens of Indian lineage. They might have been the ones already successfully integrated into our establishment. While still slightly "red" on the outside, their inside attitudes and conduct had become as white as that of their alleged exploiters. Were they, therefore, no longer identifiable as aborigines? Did they even want to be known as members of their very own distinct society? I wonder!

Had I remained in Europe, as one of the many Germans still so unusually obsessed with the plight of the Native Americans, I might have concluded my life with the quixotic fallacy about Karl May's "Noble Savages". Unfortunately I was not able to retain this illusion in the real world of aborigines that I personally experienced. I consider this very sad and—on this subject—would have preferred to remain ignorant and shielded from the real world!

MULTICULTURALISM

By the time I decided to remain in Canada, I recognized this as a bilingual and bicultural society, one founded with British traditions and based on Judeo-Christian principles. While it had been my second choice, and merely intended as an interim destination before a sponsor for the United States could be arranged, I soon came to appreciate my new environment and changed my mind about moving.

I felt then—and more importantly now—that new arrivals, wherever from, should strive to fit into the established *Franco* or *Anglo* cultures as quickly as possible. To become Canadians not merely in citizenship, but more importantly in outlook, they should give up their "damn foreigner" attitudes and strive to conduct themselves like either *Anglo* or *Franco* Canadians.

Sadly I notice while writing this that our more recent arrivals seem to be the most vociferous in insisting on changes by the country which took them in, changes by Canada to adapt to the social customs and cultural mores of these newest immigrants. And our governments of all levels accommodate and financially support such outrageous demands.

Perhaps it is my inclination to always support ferocious free-marketeering—rather than be on the side of simpering socialism—that reveals itself in my attitude toward multiculturalism. As I see it, if cultures and languages of new arrivals cannot survive in Canada under their own steam—meaning exclusively from the voluntary financial support of their own membership—they should dissolve.

When I arrived, one needed five years of residency to obtain Canadian citizenship. Both my wife and I wanted to be Canadians. We applied as early as we could. And on June 26th 1957—which was also our third wedding anniversary—we renounced German citizenship, swore allegiance to Her Majesty Queen Elizabeth the Second, and became citizens of Canada, our "Country of Choice".

It was a different Canada then. Or was it that we primarily associated with like-minded people? It seemed that most new immigrants whom we knew, quickly sought citizenship and also wanted to be *like* Canadians. All felt strongly that adjustments to be made were our responsibility. We needed to change as necessary, to help us fit into our new surroundings. We did not expect that our chosen country and its established population would adapt their ways to accommodate us.

My employment in Canada, from bases in Winnipeg, Montreal, and ultimately Toronto, exposed me constantly to foreign business communities both in Canada and abroad. But my relationship with Canada's German interests was not more intense than the commercial opportunities warranted. And to the "hyphenated" ethnic community of German immigrants I did not come closer than I was to that of India or Ireland or Italy.

I have no problem with the various demonstrations of their ethnicity by my fellow-Canadians, to which I am constantly exposed. *Caribana* celebrations; Szechuan food; *Ikebana* competitions; Ukrainian Folk Dance festivals; St.Patrick's Day parades; these all are enjoyable to a point. They are just not what, for my own ancestral ethnic group, I would promote or support or that I would want to share in as a member. No *Oktoberfest* celebrations for me!

One could imply that my eagerness to become a Canadian—and only a Canadian, never mind the hyphenated German-Canadian label—resulted primarily from my somewhat "tainted" origins. The horrific misdeeds committed during twelve years under the *swastika* banner of the Third Reich gave Germany then, and in the views of some even today, a most unsavoury reputation. This burden of collective culpability might have given those of my generation emotional and psychological reasons, not merely practical ones, to shed such a guilt-ridden former affiliation.

But is there any ethnic group, which does not have a "skeleton in the closet" about their own real or perceived abuse of others? Although the dimension of the Nazis' inhumanity towards mainly the Jews, but also against Communists, Socialists, Gypsies, Free-Masons, Homosexuals, Slavic Prisoners of War, and others who did not fit their perception of "desirables", does rank with mankind's most vicious in magnitude.

Indeed I did and always will carry the burden of this "community guilt" for the misdeeds of some of my former countrymen. Yet my urgent desire to become an "unhyphenated" Canadian was, so I hope, totally unrelated. For me, a cartoon-type German culture, with *Um-pah* music, *Lederhosen* and *Sauerkraut,* was never compatible with my life-style. The mere thought of my possible membership in an ethnic club or organization had always made me cringe.

Perhaps incorrectly, I considered such "togetherness" to be of interest only to the ethnic Germans from Eastern Europe. They had already been sufficiently punished for their German-ness with mistreatment and expulsion from their homes through "ethnic cleansing". They felt, therefore, no need for the soul-searching and repentance of those of my age who were born and raised in what remained of the former Germany, as I was.

The *Donauschwaben* had retained their German language and culture for many generations while living in the Balkans, just like the *Wolgadeutsche* did in Russia and other former Soviet Republics. As immigrants, even their second and at times their third generation Canadian-born offspring, still seem to be keenly interested in continuing their former traditions in Canada as well.

The entire concept of multiculturalism, as promoted by our federal government, strikes me as somewhat anti-Canadian. It appears to work against our struggle for the development of a coherent Canadian identity. The mere mention of our supposed *mosaic* of nationalities always reminds me of the former Yugoslavian system and its continuing problems; or the current challenges to the Russian government in Moscow. As Canadians we are, of course, too civilized to slaughter each other in a *jihad*.

But who knows, all this might just be a sinister plot that has never been mentioned by any of our politicians or even implied from one of the extreme fringes of either the sycophant or the subversive media. Only half in jest have I at times suggested that the policy for multiculturalism was really a clever scheme to denigrate French to the relative level of insignificance enjoyed by all the other non-*Anglo* cultural and language groups. Perhaps history will prove me right?

Many shortcomings that I observe in our system, and that I am forced to endure—albeit *grumblingly*—seem to be consequences of the 1982 introduction of the *Charter of Rights and Freedoms*. That's when, from my perspective at least, the dismantling of our relatively quite successful democratic system began.

Gradually, since that time, some of the government's decision-making processes have been moved away from elected officials. At least the parliamentarians could be *turfed out* in an upcoming election. But not so their totally unaccountable delegates, a gathering of judges and other "appointees", including our senators, whose previous careers—often as political hacks—had come to an end.

The continuing downloading of federal responsibilities, and the creeping abdication of any real power from the central national government to the Provinces and Territories, I dislike as well. The ultimate fear, expressed in perhaps not so humorous terms by former Prime Minister Pierre Trudeau, might well come true. He mused, as I recall, about a possible role for the Ottawa government as the mere "head waiter to the Provinces", in a Canada that was "a confederation of shopping malls".

Aren't I lucky that I am the citizen of a country where I can voice controversial opinions, without any fear of reprisal?

As Canadians, we may not live in a perfect environment either. Yet, despite these qualifying remarks, after many years of extensive international travel, I feel this today as strongly as ever. *For me*, there is no place in the world as wonderful as our own country, Canada.

They call it Discrimination

The cry of discrimination emanates from many who need to camouflage their own shortcomings. Who hasn't—and shouldn't have—experienced it at one time or other? Who doesn't discriminate himself on the odd occasion? After all, it just seems part of normal human behaviour. Not the best human conduct, but quite "normal" nevertheless. If you recognize this as a given and do not dwell on such incidents, you can get on with your life and concentrate on what is important. You might even become happy and successful.

What's so unusual about discrimination anyway? Those victimized suffer from the prejudices articulated by their fellow man simply because they are perceived as being different. In the opinion of their generalizing critics, they—usually as a group, community or organization—may be assessed as too lank, lazy, lewd, limp, loony, or loud. The list of identifiable idiosyncrasies is endless.

Yet all of a sudden, discrimination—be it real or more often imaginary—has become the favourite buzzword for the defence of the inept. Its most vociferous claimants seem to be the parasites that make a living—usually government sponsored—from the representation of the alleged sufferers. So-called "executives" of a multitude of ethnic organizations, along with immigration consultants and lawyers, are very much in the forefront as spokespersons for their "professional victims".

Complainants seem to have the full support of the professed "liberal-minded" bleeding hearts. As a centre-of-right *small-c* conservative, and an immigrant, who could well—if you stretch the point—have claimed to be "maltreated" myself, I can offer them no sympathy with their lamentations.

Was it Marshall McLuhan who described Canada as "a solution searching for a problem"? He might have been thinking of the self-important people we have today, whose constant cries of "discrimination" occupy a throng of company, labour union, and government officials; human resource staff; lawyers; and court personnel.

Whoever the most recent immigrants were, they always seemed to have been on the receiving end of good-natured or ribald ribbing from those previously established. For a current crop of greenhorns, the disparaging comments from their Canadian "elders"—not their "betters"—might relate to their ethnic, racial, cultural, social or physical characteristics.

Such discriminating critique could result from any one of a multitude of peculiarities. Their different attire; the food they prepare and its resultant smell during cooking; their diet's impact on body odour; their limited linguistic capabilities or peculiar accents; their loud public conversations in strange sounding foreign languages; their excessive display of demonstrative mannerisms; their males' attitude towards women; the way they deal with their offspring; their reaction to authority figures; even the way they vote.

Can you blame a landlord, for not approving of a tenant who regularly cooks elaborate meals with unusual odoriferous foods and strange spices; or accuse an employer for not hiring the applicant whose linguistic abilities do not meet the job requirements? Indeed, wouldn't you suffer, at least silently, while working next to someone who reeks of strange scents; or regularly interrupts his work schedule to meet his religious requirements? Without resentment, could you stand in a line-up next to some folks pushing, gesticulating and conversing loudly in a foreign tongue?

As a newcomer, should you really be offended by hearing the term chink, coon, dago, gook, nig-nog, paki or ragtop applied to you now? Could this offend you any more than fifty years ago, at the height of one of the waves of European immigration, when you might have been called a frog, honky, kike, kraut, limey, mick, polack or wop? Even the term *D.P.* was used in a derogatory way at the time of my own immigration. The perfectly acceptable abbreviation for *Displaced Person*, it seemed to be tagged disparagingly as an identifier to anyone who arrived from Continental Europe.

We do live, after all, in a country of immigrants. The mere difference is that some of us or our ancestors arrived earlier than did others. Yet, no matter how hard you try to fit in as an immigrant yourself—rather than as the descendant of one—you will always encounter strange questions. Every now and then, a native-born Canadian may want to get back to uncovering your roots—that you might have considered to be well camouflaged—with a "No, really, where *do* you come from? I mean, *originally*".

You were not born in your chosen country, and, therefore, you will always be different from the locals. That remains despite your best efforts to assimilate by dressing, moving, and eating like a Canadian; your illusion that you have reduced or eliminated your foreign accent; even the ultimate conversion by assuming an anglicized name. No matter how much you wave the Canadian flag, some will always perceive your Canadian-ness as an overcoat, with the original foreigner still underneath. But, surely, none of this has anything to do with prejudice or discrimination!

You may belong to what we now call a *visible minority*, rather than being endowed with a pale or grey or pink—even a brown—complexion, which are the true hues of those classified as "white". Yet, with our current crop of immigrants arriving almost exclusively from Third World countries and their attendant high birth rates, at least in their first generation, describing them as "minorities" may soon prove to be a misnomer.

So being black or yellow is surely no longer a hindrance to an impressive career. Quite the contrary may be true. Initially, it might well have taken *Affirmative Action* programs to open doors that were previously not accessible. But today, when some large organizations still struggle to have at least one token black or brown or aborigine on their Board of Directors or with their Senior Management team, people of colour at times receive preferred consideration—assuming, of course, that they have the basic qualifications.

Any reports of supposed discrimination that came to my attention during over fifty years in Canada have usually been anecdotal. In some cases I just couldn't "get the point" of the perceived defamation. For a few I saw the humour rather than the offence in a particular critical statement. On some others I even agreed with the alleged perpetrator of the discriminatory action against the—in my opinion—deserving victim.

I recall but two such incidents of offensive remarks being applied to me personally. Yet not then nor ever since have I considered them "discriminatory".

In my capacity as the head of an employer's operations in Montreal, I was once confronted by one of the firm's drivers, who had been fired—"for cause" as even the Teamsters Labour Union steward would finally have to concur. This dismissed employee was not satisfied with the stern explanations of his foreman or with the soothing words of the warehouse superintendent. He wanted to air his grievance with "the big boss". When he physically threatened me in my own office, he accompanied his utterances with extensive verbal abuse concerning my ethnic background.

This was an altogether new experience. Right to my face, no one had ever heaped insults on me because of my ancestry. Of course, what might have been said behind my back by others, I never knew, and I didn't care. Self-deprecating humour, poking fun at myself and at people like me—including ethnic Germans—had always seemed amusing. And, in this area, I never objected to any good-natured ribbing from others, either.

The second occurrence that I might have considered as "serious" was some twenty-five years after the first incident, when my German ethnic background again gave cause for derogatory comments. It happened at a private farewell party for one of my former associates. Hardly a person without intellect, he was a Professional Engineer and had served as a Canadian military officer during the liberation of Europe in WW2.

By the time he made his revelation he had been extensively into the freely provided Scotch. In a very civilized manner he approached me privately and quietly to announce his real views. He had been able to conceal these throughout our close professional relationship some years before, during his temporary tenure as an effective manager in one of the international offices, which I administered at the time. Now he felt free to state that—so he emphasized—while he had treated me with the respect due a man with my position during our working life, he nevertheless always thought of me as a "fucking Kraut".

Good old chap! Wasn't it fortunate that he displayed some civility in the manner in which he presented his views, and that I had a sense of humour. Otherwise one of us might have ruined a perfectly good party.

Childhood exposure to frequent slurs concerning my unusual reddish hair colour had well prepared me for critique from strangers. As a youngster, I was often ridiculed and thereby suffered greatly. Being called a *Rotfuchs* or Red Fox was the ultimate insult for someone with my predicament in the region where I grew up. And it was only because, for the longest time, I personally considered this a handicap—something, which made me "inferior" to others, so I thought—that I felt abused. But since my maturity, only my immediate family and those few friends, whom I consider to be particularly close to me, could ever hurt my feelings. Statements by others I would ignore quite easily.

My advice for recent immigrants, who feel that they are singled out for ridicule or (Give me a break!) for "persecution", is therefore to shrug it off and to be patient. In time it will surely go away. Yet, until these new fellow-Canadians have developed a thicker skin and, above all, acquired the conviction that they are *not* inferior, they might also be well advised to recall the advice I wish my parents had given to me as a child. It ultimately became my "You can't argue with an idiot" philosophy.

ISLAMISTS AMONG US

We face an enormous challenge as a nation and as a civilization—not as a race or a religion, so I must emphasize. It is our clash with something as financially powerful from oil money as the Islamist movement.

Its fundamentalist adherents might well be a minute number from among practicing or hereditary Muslims. Yet, however small this component, they are a danger to us all. And the more militant among their *mullahs* and *imams* reportedly gain converts to their cause in ever-growing numbers—even in the Western world.

Our own countrymen with such a background—if they are of this fanatical breed—instead of wanting to become Canadians beyond the entitlement to a passport, might instead be longing for the days when Baghdad and the Arab world were centres of civilization. They were deprived of this predominance when their area was overrun by Europe's barbarian Crusaders, and later again by the terrifying Mongols. Some of the then subdued—evolving into today's fundamentalists—lost their original role of leadership but retained their medieval social practices.

Wisely, perhaps, the hordes from the eastern steppes eventually converted to Islam and helped spread its message to other parts of the world. The Europeans, however, missed their chance to return home with the "true faith". They limited their new-found adaptations to the Arabs'—at that time—more civilized customs and advanced discoveries.

I hate to generalize, or—worse still—stereotype *à la Hollywood*. Yet I fear that some of our current imports—if they retain their medieval social culture's tribal bigotry and do not help stop or at least sincerely and vigorously condemn the fundamentalists—may never fit into Canada's traditional establishment. They could succeed where their ancestors had failed in most of Europe, by changing our existing environment to the point where we have to mesh into theirs.

Had they earlier been successful with the conversion of Europe, then, by extension, North America and other former European colonial outlets would have become part of the Islamic world as well. This might have spared us from today's controversies and avoided the evolving "Clash of Civilizations". Instead

41

we could then present our Confession of Faith, the *Shahada,* in the original Arabic. Just like the many millions of practicing Muslims who, throughout their lives, recite it five times each day, as

Ashadu an
La ilaha il Allah
Muhammad-ur-Rasool-Allah
(I bear witness
None has the right to be worshipped but Allah
And Muhammad is the messenger of Allah).

As the religion seems *intended,* my reaction to Islam, after extensive reading on the *true faith* of the movement, has often been positive. As a believer in any Higher Power—which I am not—I could find their views, that Abraham, Moses, Jesus and Muhammad were all prophets of the same God, even more plausible than the categorical assertions by many other faiths.

Yet one cannot reason with those pervaded by a twisted interpretation of this or any other religion. Radical Islamists claim, for the guidance and inspiration of angry and resentful adherents, that complete happiness—and a bevy of beautiful virgins yet—awaits each of them in the *Gardens of Al-Firdaus* (paradise). Just as long as they slaughter any of their real or perceived enemies along with themselves! I could not find such commands anywhere in the *Qur'an.* However, it is the alleged belief of some fanatics.

Such mutants of humanity are not likely to prescribe to a directive for combat attributed to General Patton, to "let the other dumb bastard die for *his* country". Since they have no fear of perishing themselves, there may be no way to stop their mayhem with conventional means—ever.

To help build bridges of understanding, I am making every effort to get to know Muslims. I cannot call any of them my "personal friends" as yet. But I try. Claims of discrimination, which I shrug off as a crutch for the unqualified; multiculturalism, which I abhor as a demonstration by the incompatible; and my yet unfulfilled desire to visit a Mosque, which I pursue with sincerity; are usually good introductory themes for a lively exchange.

The operator of a restaurant, where we visit regularly; two owners of small businesses that I frequent; some limousine drivers from the airport (in T.O. many are well-educated Muslims or Sikhs, so it seems); and my chats with total strangers whom I encounter in line-ups or in other "holding patterns"; often provide appropriate conversation partners for an interesting discourse. So far, none revealed themselves with *Islamist* views.

The *Qur'an*, with N. J. Dawood's stimulating translation (Penguin Classics, The Koran, 1956), provides direction in Sure 3:118, when it tells its faithful:

Believers,
do not make friends with any but your own people.
They will spare no pains to corrupt you.
They desire nothing but your ruin.
Their hatred is evident from what they utter with their mouths,
but greater is the hatred which their breasts conceal.

With this in mind, would a fanatic fundamentalist really try to humour me, an obvious *infidel*, by pretending to be "objective"—from my Western perception—rather than cursing me and my kind, or at least glaring at me maliciously?

Fortunately, so far, instead of any antipathy, I discovered that their interests, aspirations and concerns were quite identical to mine. So just like Nazis ruined the world's perception of all Germans, with similarly absurd slogans and evil deeds, the violent misfits among Muslims do such harm to their entire community as well.

There are probably as many variations of Islam, as there are flavours of Christianity. Despite my background in the latter faith, I would be hard-pressed to justify, from a religious angle, the continuing struggle between the opposing nutcases in Ireland. Most Muslims might be similarly challenged with an evaluation of their Islamists' cause.

I frequently encountered members of the Sikh religion, which I consider as a derivative of Islam—possibly over objections from some of their adherents. I also had occasional contact with Ismailies, whom I heard described as perhaps the most westernized of the Muslim groups. In a professional environment, I was able to assess my contacts as very sophisticated people. Those representing other Islamic sub-units, with whom I had personal encounters to date, also professed to approach controversial subjects with an open mind.

Yet the politically-correct bleeding-heart liberal components of all levels of government and of our society in general try to persuade me that my views and concerns about Islamists are totally unacceptable. Our entire "race industry" would brand my thoughts as discriminatory, racist and perverse—derogatory interpretations of my feelings that had never occurred to me.

For how much longer will I be able to voice my opinion and reveal myself as an *infidel* without any fear of reprisal? Might I be "living dangerously" even in the allegedly *enlightened* Canada of the 21st century?

A Kraut Despite it All

Ich sit *an meinem* desk *mit* pen *und* paper *und* write *einen* letter. This is close to the style in which a few of my former countrymen express themselves, when they use their native German. They claim to have forgotten much of their first language, although they came to Canada as adults.

I don't believe it! It is either a put-on in a vain attempt to impress their friends and relations from the old country; or perhaps an indication of a never overcome affliction with a very limited intellect. While observing the main offenders, I usually note that their level of sophistication in the allegedly more familiar second language, English, is nothing they can brag about, either.

It is understandable that one misses the occasional word. After my fifty years in Canada, there are newly coined German expressions of which even I, despite my frequent travels to Europe, am unaware. These did not yet exist when I emigrated. But how can anyone lose the knowledge of a language, with which he or she grew up?

At times I, too, draw on English words in my *Deutsch*; or German terms when I speak English. It is usually for special effect, and not because I get mixed up. I might say that "Ich *bonde* mit meinen Enkeln". This English expression I apply, because I have not yet discovered a German equivalent to effectively describe the relationship with my grandchildren that I constantly try to advance. In an English dialogue, I actually use Yiddish variations of the original German terms that I acquired right here in Canada, if I state my affection for a person with "He is a real *Mensch*" or identify another by his colour with "This chap is a *Schwarzes*".

I really consider myself a Canadian, and *only* a Canadian. I make this point again and again. None of that hyphenated German-Canadian stuff for me. No doubt this greatly amuses—perhaps, because of its nauseating repetitiveness, even annoys—my Canadian-born acquaintances. Chances are that some may forever think of me as a German—although not necessarily a *bloody Kraut*.

My spouse and I will always consider our family's first Canadian-born offspring, our son, as our greatest achievement in life. Through Ken and his wife Birte, our three Canadian-by-birth grandchildren will, so I dare hope and expect, continue the line and the family tradition in what originally became Gussie's and my country of choice.

Birte keeps reminding me occasionally that two of the little darlings were born in Denmark, and even the youngest, a native of Oakville/Ontario, is Danish by birth as well. Should we agree then that they are 50% Canadian and Danish each? And—my eternal hope—that Canada will always be their homeland!

Becoming a Canadian, for me, was a serious endeavour. It proved to have been the right thing to do. And *still* I am also a German, eh! For some people I am, anyway. But what do I care? Or do I? I must, otherwise why would I be whining with this little sermon?

AMERICANS ARE MY FRIENDS

Most of the time, Americans are Canada's very best friends. Even on the rare occasions when, temporarily, they are not, they *should* be—despite any professed ideological clashes between the two nations. During such episodes, our "leaders" seem to disagree primarily on the methods applied, even if their aims and objectives are identical. Fortunately, for both countries, the business communities and the public in general are more attuned.

Perhaps I should clarify that, more often than not, I feel it is *our* gang of elected "sages", which does not fit. I really doubt if the U.S. administration, particularly the White House, ever gave us too much thought before the divergence of views about Iraq. According to a media report—now don't ask me when and where this was—President Bush nicknamed our long-overdue-for-retirement Prime Minister Chrétien as "dino"—short for *dinosaur* no doubt. I hope that, with such a label, the American authorities can shrug off the regularly displayed anti-American antics of the current Ottawa regime, which might soon be replaced and, therefore, is "no longer pertinent".

My earliest contact with Americans was indirect. I observed their flying aircraft from the ground below, when they operated their bombing missions over Hitler's Germany during the Second World War. I also noted the impact of their explosives on my surroundings. Not once did I reflect on how I might have felt about these chaps trying to kill me. They were the enemy alright, but—perhaps it was because of my tender age—I never thought of them that way.

After the end of hostilities, when our original invaders, the French, evacuated the area where I lived and it became part of the U.S. Occupation Zone, I had my first face-to-face encounter with the Americans. Their soldiers appeared like other young men in uniform, but more jovial and less formal than the German or the French military I had experienced earlier. They also were the bearers and gracious distributors of many of the goodies that I wanted to scrounge—or that I sought to trade with them in my later black-market transactions.

The evident material wealth that one naively observed, even among the army's foot soldiers, and the suspected affluence of friends and relations who lived in the USA and sent food parcels to their German relations, seemed awesome. Years later I learned that my mother's American cousins were not wealthy at all. These kind-hearted and sincerely religious people were able to bestow such occasional benefits on us, because they economized in other areas. They even endured the occasional verbal abuse from their fellow-countrymen, when, at the post office, they dispatched the parcels to their recently defeated *bloody Kraut* relations.

My experiences as a youngster confirmed that, if American, it *had* to be good. This was the general perception by many of my contemporaries immediately after the war. I still recall one particular media story of the time. An assumed food parcel, received by a—real or invented—German family, held a metal container with a powdery substance. The undernourished recipients tasted and ultimately consumed it, mistaking it for powdered soup. A notice, delayed in transit, eventually revealed that these had been the ashes of a recently departed family member. "If it is American it tastes good, even if it is the very own grandmother" was the headline of this perhaps fictitious report.

Some of my friends and I really went to extremes in an effort to imitate our occupiers. As teenagers, we mimicked the American GIs as much as we could. We rarely sat without putting our feet on a table or desk; and chewing gum became a constant habit; in my case, to my parents' great annoyance.

Expressions like *OK, Thanks, Hi* and *Bye;* or an appreciative *Hubba-Hubba;* as well as expletives not quite suitable for use in mixed company; became part of one's German vocabulary. The only music to which I listened attentively was American, to the particular dismay of my father. Every product advertised in an American magazine was an article of great desire. The ultimate dream for many was to emigrate to the U.S. of A.

My hometown had an *America House*, established for the "conversion" of the young and the otherwise receptive among the recently defeated. It became one of my frequent hangouts. Where applied to me personally, the efforts of the occupiers, to win the hearts and minds of former enemies, were indeed a success. *Amerikahaus* is where I learned a fair bit about their country, beyond the limited perceptions that the German author Karl May, in his writings about their "Noble Savages", had instilled in me during my childhood.

Movies shown immediately after the war were all Hollywood-made. One that I remember clearly was *Tom, Dick and Harry.* It became memorable only because it was the first feature film screened in my hometown for a German audience—not because it was that good a show.

Once I had savoured my very first hamburger and milkshake, I was completely converted. For this memorable event, a couple of my friends and I were the guests of one Fred L. Miller and his wife, from Kansas City. In their new *Buick,* they drove us for a visit to Heidelberg, where the outing concluded with a snack in the Americans' cafeteria.

Mr. Miller was administrator of the school system for the children of American personnel in Germany. Through him and his wife, I had my initial exposure to a private home of American civilians. They revealed themselves as kind and considerate people—religious, without being fanatical, and much more charitable than I experienced over the years of my extensive international travel among many other cultures. In my entire life in North America since then, I discovered most of the contacts in their country, with whom I established a closer personal relationship, as equally friendly, warm-hearted and helpful.

My initial target for emigration had been the United States. However, without the required sponsorship, I arrived as an immigrant in Canada instead—just temporarily, so I thought when I came here in 1951. Once a move to the States became a possibility, I was already sufficiently enthralled with the opportunities in Canada, to remain and make it my country of choice forever. The likelihood of a stint in the U.S. military—they had a draft system, Canada did not—may also have been a discouraging factor.

Extensive exposure to all our Provinces, and my frequent travels through every one of their States, let me declare categorically that they were indeed "our type of people". Some of my countrymen regularly moan that Americans do not have our universal health care system but own handguns instead, which—so the complainants proclaim—supposedly makes us a "kinder and gentler society". *Really?*

For reasons of their own—political opportunism, perhaps—generations of our politicians, at intervals, profess their feelings of anti-Americanism. Minor segments of the public, and more often the academic elites, do this for their own mundane motives. They do not speak on my behalf!

We always benefited from our southern neighbours' commercial power; as they did from many of our natural and human resources. Throughout the last century, with our oldest and most frequent allies, the British, we used to be among those who led the way in global conflicts against tyranny, long before our American friends became involved. In recent years, however, we have been sponging off the Americans' military might—just like most other countries of the Western Alliance, with the *Brits* being the honourable exception.

Without the Americans' participation in the Second World War and thereafter, today's considerably anti-American *Continentals* would no doubt "thrive" under a fascist or a communist dictatorship. As democratic governments go, the Yanks remain as "the best game around". Charitable support for *the great unwashed*, to friends and foes alike, they still provide generously. Their approach to business—despite some recent malfunctions of the capitalist system—and the way in which they always encourage personal initiative, impress me no end.

I could go on indefinitely. Yet you can also select any one of my admiring statements and give rebuttals for something that has gone wrong through an American initiative.

One such "to the contrary" illustration applies to Afghanistan. Without American support against the occupying Soviet forces, the country might still be under a—to us today—relatively harmless communist regime. Such a dictatorship would have "neutralized" (by torture, expulsion or outright murder) the dissidents *within* their own borders and—much to our benefit—helped purge some of the religious fanatics that evolved into the *Al-Qaeda* movement of 9/11-fame. This would surely have spared us the later battle against the Taliban forces, and eradicated many of the Islamic fundamentalists, who form the backbone of today's terrorism squads.

The same critique could apply to relations with Iraq's Saddam Hussein, who, when he fought the Iranians, was a great friend and deserving the full support of the United States. Then—for, to me, still rather nebulous reasons—he became an enemy; although, throughout his years in power, his dictatorial regime seemed to have frowned on religious fanaticism, the apparent root cause of today's terrorism.

If we accepted the invasion of Iraq by the USA as a legitimate endeavour, we would surely have to applaud any attack on Pakistan by India as an equally justifiable "pre-emptive strike".

However, none of these ultimate calamities alter the overall picture. As today's only superpower, they may not be perfect. Who could be, in this not always envious position? Surely not the Russians, the Chinese or—what a horrifying thought—the Arabs. Americans consider theirs as the greatest nation on earth; and, once aware of all their blessings, who would ever have the effrontery to try to change *their* views?

On the Canadian scene, for much of the past century or two, our reaction to their overpowering presence was conditioned by our quest for a separate national identity. Just because the Americans are so like us—most notably with an *almost* common language and a heretofore, albeit gradually eroding, Judeo-Christian value system in both our countries—we have a legitimate apprehension that they could simply swallow us up. Americans, typically, have no conception why this might be a problem for Canada.

We do indeed have a great deal to lose. Without—as we sing in our national anthem—"standing on guard" for our cherished traditions and our somewhat different way of life, we could well dissolve completely into an American orbit. Therefore, when I reiterate that Americans, as individuals, are mostly very nice people, and that I admire them as a nation, I must also emphasize that I want to remain a Canadian. Particularly since, as an independent country, we seem to have fared better for ourselves doing most of the things that matter *to us* in "our way".

However, let me get back to basics. In relative terms for population size and international significance, we compare to the USA, as Denmark relates to Germany. "In their hearts", I do not think that Danes are particularly fond of their Teutonic neighbours to the South. Yet they can take comfort from many moderating influences against being culturally overpowered and ultimately absorbed. They speak an entirely different language; have more European nations sharing their continent as a counterbalance; enjoy somewhat dissimilar priorities in lifestyle; and, above all, benefit from the reality that Denmark's commercial interdependence with the Germans is much less momentous than our own is so almost exclusively with the Americans. Nevertheless—at least publicly—they treat the "*poelse tysker*" (sausage Germans) with respect! They consider this wise. Unlike some of our presently empowered Liberal politicians; as well as the "also-rans" of our Socialist hordes; and various Separatists in Quebec; who regularly mutter about the "ugly and (so they accuse them currently) war-mongering Americans".

With their so often self-absorbed concerns and views of *their very own* universe—we usually benefited from the Americans' "benign neglect". I hope, therefore, that our southern relations, close neighbours, frequent allies and biggest trading partners—now that, because of Iraq, we have come under their scrutiny—will either eventually forget, or magnanimously ignore, our sporadic eccentricities. At least they should know that I—along with most of my Canadian compatriots, so I dare hope—always consider them kindly and admiringly as our very best friends!

RELIGION

On the first day of January in 1930, I was baptized in Karlsruhe's *Liebfrauen-kirche.* This was the church where my parents had been married on March 7th 1925, also in a Roman Catholic ceremony.

As a small child I spent many of my days in the *Canisius Haus Kindergarten,* the Nursery School closest to our home. It was run by Catholic nuns, who, I would assume—although I do not specifically recollect this—must have provided some religious inspiration to their young charges.

In the *Uhland Volksschule* (Grade School, from age 6 to 10), we had one hour twice each week, when our class divided into Catholics (Roman Catholic that is) and Protestants (all these were Lutheran) for enlightenment by priests or pastors of these respective faiths.

The *Kant Oberrealschule* (my High School from age ten until close to the end of the war when I was fifteen), also taught *Religion*. By then we segregated into three groups, the third one with a membership of those classified as *Gottgläubig.* While the word translates as "believers in god" this was actually meant for non-believers, whose parents did not want them exposed to the teachings of any faith—other than that of the ruling Nazi party, perhaps.

As a family we went to church on all the important Catholic holidays. For a while, particularly leading up to my *First Holy Communion* at age ten, I always attended Sunday Mass. I continued with this routine for some months after I had been so "anointed" when, after going to Confession the day before, I regularly took Communion.

I still remember the probing questions of one or two of the priests in the con-fessional cubicles, as they dealt with my real or imaginary sexual encounters. I also recall the secrets that I did not reveal to them during these embarrassing interrogations.

Most of my friends were Lutheran by upbringing. No one ever said this, I am certain, but somehow I had the impression that, as a Catholic, I would surely be struck by lightning if I ever entered a Protestant church. *Ergo,* I did not.

My summer vacations were usually spent with distant relatives on a farm. The entire community was Catholic. All I retained from one Sunday's sermon—it must have been at the time of the battle for Stalingrad—was the foolishly daring choice of words by the village priest. He said that Napoleon, too, had successfully marched in Russia, until he finally lost the war. Shortly thereafter, this *Pfarrer* disappeared, no doubt on the recommendation of a local Nazi, who had denounced him to the authorities.

The last church service for me—I almost made it, but not quite—was together with my parents on Christmas Eve that same year. My father must have been on leave from the military at the time. When we arrived for the *Christmette*, the Midnight Mass, the church was already too crowded for us to be admitted. I quickly returned home in a huff, while my Mom and Dad did their rituals in the lobby of the edifice. Thereafter, my parents never again prodded me to go to church.

Once I resumed my schooling after the war, we were back into two separate groups of the allegedly faithful for an hour each week of *Religionsunterricht*. The "non-believers" among us were excused during these time slots. Perhaps I should have joined them, because, for total lack of interest, Religion was not one of my better subjects.

Since my mid-teens, I already considered myself an Agnostic. I did a fair bit of reading on different religions. The *Bahai* movement was something I briefly considered as a worthy pursuit. Later, after I became a "militant non-smoker", I thought that *Sikhs*, with their views about tobacco consumption, had at least one routine that turned me on. *Judaism*, as a possible option, interested me greatly, because of my inherent ancestral guilt complex about the mistreatment of Jews throughout history; although their prescribed circumcision would eventually have discouraged me—I can feel the pain just thinking about it.

Gussie had a Lutheran background. We were married in *St. John's Lutheran Church* in Montreal. Years later, for the benefit of our son, we often attended their services, and Kenneth was baptized there as well. On and off, even after we moved to Ontario, we went to church.

While I frequently travelled abroad on business, Gussie took our son to Sunday services as well. Yet Kenneth never had his "Confirmation", which is the Lutherans' ceremony for fourteen-year olds, so I have been advised.

The very few of our friends, who are indeed religious, kept "praying for me" over many years. Perhaps they still are. Some always hoped that they could re-convert me to Christianity. They expressed amazement that—so they stated—someone as "kind and good and clean-living" as I *appeared* to them (the italics are *mine*), could be such *without* a deep faith. They were unsuccessful, of course. But we are still friends!

For a while, a Lutheran Minister was one of our neighbours. We attended his church occasionally and—under duress, so I felt—ultimately also participated in an evening class which he conducted for a "mature audience". The unquestioning acceptance and the child-like profession of faith by the adult participants, and the general mumbo-jumbo of the topic as a whole, made me wince. While I joined this group as a mere *agnostic*, I finished up as an *atheist*.

I don't recall ever having been very devout. I merely observed the various rituals with which I had been indoctrinated. Once I had progressively advanced—or deteriorated, depending on the point of view—to the end of my religious phase, I never experienced a crisis of conscience. Whatever "true" faith I might have had before, if any, just withered away.

I have no problem with the religious orientation of others. I myself grew up—and still try to live accordingly—in a "slightly religious" household with a Judeo-Christian orientation. For many, of whatever persuasion, the teachings of their faiths may indeed have made them better people. I even envy those who, with some tragedy in their family—a terminal illness, for example—can put their "trust in God", cheerfully accepting the suffering and expecting their rewards in a later life. This is just not for me!

For purely academic reasons—nothing to do with religious fervour—I recently read the Bible. Christians generally refer to it as "the Old Testament", so I learned. Since I frequently interrupted this with the perusal of more current literature on other subjects, it became a lengthy project. The tome encompasses some 800 pages in rather small print. While I had never studied it before, there was little of significance that I had not heard described in subdued variations on many earlier occasions.

With this scrutiny of the full text of the Bible, however, I became greatly disturbed by the violence promoted and the vicious retributions, which an allegedly benevolent God ordered as punishment for even minor infractions to his proclaimed ordinances. I also found it remarkable to detect the cavalier way in which the Almighty, as the distributor of this part of *his* world, covered or ignored the obvious fate of the earlier inhabitants of the designated "Promised Land". His ultimate direction to the territory's invaders seemed to be to *exterminate* the locals. An early form of ethnic cleansing, I suspect.

My next literary pursuit was a re-reading of the New Testament, something to which—in a Christian upbringing—I had been exposed extensively. With this I made no new discoveries.

To culminate my venture into "the Good Books", I currently very much enjoy my exposure to the Qur'an. Of course, this is in translation. Hopefully it is an

English version that would find approval among the faith's current Imams, since I am not planning to learn Arabic to absorb the prophet's recollection of Allah's wisdom in the original language.

Of all the religious writings that I encountered, there is little I found more moving than my recent discovery of the poetic revelation of the *Fatiha*, again with the translation by N. J. Dawood, as my introduction to the Qur'an. To spare you, my reader, a search in a library or on the web, I will record it here:

> *In the name of God, the Merciful, the Compassionate*
> *Praise belongs to God, Lord of all Being*
> *The All-merciful, the All-compassionate*
> *The Master of the Day of Doom*
> *Thee only we serve, to Thee alone we pray for succour*
> *Guide us in the straight path*
> *The path of those whom Thou hast blessed*
> *Not of those against whom Thou art wrathful*
> *Nor of those who are astray.*

I do not seek to be converted; and have no interest in rediscovering my old faith, or becoming attracted to a new one. My continuing visits to churches, temples or shrines are totally without religious overtones. I either view them as interesting edifices, from the perspective of a tourist; or I conform to our civilization's traditions by attending baptisms, weddings and funerals.

My parents were somewhat disturbed by my comments during one of my many visits from Canada. I told them that—in my assessment—they had always lived good Christian lives in the *Protestant* tradition, and not at all like *Roman Catholics*, which they thought they were.

Yet both had their burial routine in accordance with their perceived faith. Mother, as the surviving spouse, pre-planned her funeral in minute detail. With many of our immediate family in attendance, we concluded this day—long into the early morning hours—with a jolly good party in Mom's apartment; one that she would have enjoyed immensely, had she been with us in person and not just in our fond memories.

I always thought that a Viking funeral would have been a magnificent event. Placed on a combustible vessel, once this was set on fire, the so honoured would be sent out to sea by family and friends, all of them totally inebriated, of course. What a way to go! But, since this would be rather expensive to conduct, and—from an environmentalist's standpoint—might be totally unacceptable, I'll just have to settle for the next best thing.

My own final exit should, therefore, proceed in accordance with my new-found faith—or rather my conviction *not* to have one. There are to be no religious rites to commemorate my ultimate departure; and no display and visitation at a funeral parlour, either. I always considered the viewing of "the dearly beloved" in an *open* casket a particularly barbaric custom and an imposition on the attendees, who had come "to pay their respects". And it was a horror of horrors how I perceived the ritual of some cultures, which forces children to kiss the corpses of their relations on the mouth.

There will be none of these macabre performances when I go, not even a funeral. But I would not object—how could I, anyway, since I will be "the departed"—to a gathering for a merry bash, where the attendants smile, or, better still, roar with laughter, recalling some of our happy encounters over the years.

THE FESTIVE SEASON

Hanukkah is the Jewish *Festival of Lights*; *Eid al Fitr* the celebration for Muslims to commemorate the end of *Ramadan;* this year both at about the same time. North American Blacks—I should call ours Afro-Canadians, of course—observe what they have identified as their very own day, something they call *Kwanzaa*. Let's not forget *Diwali* for our Hindu countrymen and, who knows what else, that Canadians observe around Christmas.

When I was a child I grew up with *Weihnacht*, to be celebrated in December. The word translates into "Sanctified" or "Blessed Night", a more neutral term in the original German. My fellow-Canadians of other persuasions might consider this less controversial than the more categorical English-language word *Christ*mas that *politically correct* activists among us seem to reject.

One has to watch out for these things! I just learned that Gary Doer, current Premier of Manitoba, has reinstated "Christmas Tree" to describe what they erect annually in the rotunda of the Provincial Assembly in Winnipeg. Good for him! His overly concerned predecessors had converted it to a—for me somewhat nauseating—"Multicultural Tree" since 1990.

I am not religious. That's why, when questioned for the census survey, I used to list myself with "no religion". But I have changed my declaration—albeit not my religious abstinence—and now insist on appearing as "Christian"; even as "Roman Catholic", should amplification be required. After all, this is my cultural background, and it is culturally that I want to help counterbalance the overwhelming numbers of our more recent immigrants from other civilizations, who take their varied creeds more seriously than I do mine.

The greetings I convey at this time of year have also changed. To accommodate everyone, I had gently been brainwashed into saying the politically correct "Happy Holidays", a nebulous and inoffensive statement. Yet, since one now seems to force me to be non-controversial, I have reverted with vigour to "Merry Christmas". I would even consider "Happy Hanukkah", but won't go beyond this in my efforts to avoid offending anyone during *my civilization's* Christmas-time.

I recently noticed a lapel button, inscribed "Jesus called, he wants his religion back". My point exactly!

Until a couple of decades ago, ours was a country with a population of primarily European ancestry, living under mainly British traditions and in a Judeo-Christian culture. Arrivals from other environments—to better assimilate themselves or more easily integrate their children, if for no other reason—tried to adjust or convert to our civilization. This is no more!

Whatever else the minority—soon no doubt the majority—of these newer Canadians do, for me and for my family it is Christmas that we celebrate. Of course, when, throughout the year, I become aware of another culture's special day, and then encounter someone who might qualify, I most certainly wish them a "Happy/Happy"—whatever it is.

The German tradition, with which I grew up, had Christmas Eve, the 24th, as the most significant component. The tree could not be set up and decorated until that afternoon; the presents were given out—depending on the age of the youngsters in the household—either before or after the evening meal; and then my family attended the *Christmette* in the local Roman-Catholic church. Both the 25th and the 26th, as the first and the second *Weihnachtstag*, were public holidays. The decorations remained until after January 6th. A *Krippe* (*crèche* or manger, highlighting the Baby Jesus) under our tree was always part of the display.

As aspiring "true blue" Canadians, we wanted to delay the presentation of our son's gifts until the morning of Christmas Day. Yet, after Kenneth had become old enough to associate the concept of the *Weihnachtsmann* with new toys, we did this for the very last time. He couldn't sleep that night, and neither did we, his parents. Every few minutes he would get up, to investigate if Santa Claus had arrived as yet. So much for our efforts to do things in the British tradition! It seemed to us that, for this one at least, the Germans had a better arrangement.

With three grandchildren, Christmas now seems even more important and enjoyable than ever. Our decorations, including the tree, come out for the first Sunday of Advent. One of the displays is an *Adventskranz* (wreath), with the four candles to be lit in sequence during each of the four *Advent*-Sundays leading up to the festival.

On one of these Sundays, we also join our children to drink *Gloegg*, a—I am certain it is fortified with *Aquavit*—heated red wine with raisins and almonds added. We also eat *aebleskiver,* small hole-of-the-donut-type fried things, for which I, in my extremely limited Danish, invented the description *Jule Boller*, or Christmas Balls. Needless to say, my daughter-in-law's relations are no doubt the only Danes, who recognize this novel terminology. These *J/Bs* we dip into sugar and jam. It makes for yummy snacking!

Our tree is artificial and has electric bulbs. In recent years we used only its top half. While this results in a shorter tree, it also reduces my workload in setting it up.

The kids have a natural tree. In what must be a Scandinavian tradition, it is decorated with miniature Danish flags. In addition to many other decorations and strings of tiny electric lights—it also has real candles. I seem to be the only one apprehensive about this. Whenever the wax candles are lit, I ensure that I have the car keys in my pocket, stand reasonably close to the exit, and know exactly where to find my grandchildren, to quickly evacuate them to safety, should there be an emergency.

Part of the Danish practice is for all of us to hold hands and "dance" around the tree. This is combined with the singing of various carols. Most of these I recognize as appropriate for the season, from both their English and their German editions. But—not aware of the background—I found two of them rather unusual for the time of year.

I knew these Christmas songs for Scandinavian children as somewhat raucous ditties in *Brigandedeutsch,* the peculiar lingo of my birthplace Karlsruhe. The Danish Christmas version talks about a *Nissen*—one of their goblins—as sitting in the attic with his rice pudding or, in the original text *"Paa loftet sidder nissen med sin julegroed".* As a child I had learned to memorize the tune as *"Der Vadder gehd der Mudder mit der Wixberschd noch"*, reporting that Dad runs after Mom with a polishing brush. The second tune, in the German version, declares how "we'll get drunk on the proceeds from the sale of Grandma's little house". No such proclamation in the Danish version.

For my grandchildren, a particularly memorable tune during these festivities might well remain the one that always made me jump off the floor, while we circled around the tree. The only word I recognized, "hop", repeated in the Danish text of this song, induced me to holler and really *hop* two feet high. Well, perhaps somewhat less—would you believe three inches off the ground?

Needless to say that—just as we did with our son—for their parents to eventually get a good night's sleep, our grandchildren's presents, and those for the rest of the family, are distributed on Christmas Eve. This is delayed until after the sumptuous and lengthy meal. For the little ones, of course, it is pure torture to sit at the dinner table, with the many unopened packages displayed underneath the tree.

The culinary delights presented are always a real Scandinavian gourmet feast that Birte arranges. The "Canadian" component—has it become global by now?—is always the turkey; and Gussie brings along her home-cooked squash, a vegetable taste we acquired from our Algonquian Indians.

The traditional dessert of rice pudding contains a single whole almond, the finder of which receives a special present—in Denmark, so I am told, usually a marzipan piggy. Since at least one of my grandchildren would never eat marzipan, this cannot be the reward during our family's routine.

For Christmas Day, the family congregates at our house. On this occasion, Gussie serves ham and an extensive variety of delicious extras.

Some day I might again be able to enjoy goose as the main course. That's what my mother prepared for Christmas Day. But then, there were only the three of us. And a goose is hardly sufficient food for seven people. I'll just have to order this in a restaurant, on one of my future visits to Germany.

At Christmas—indeed, throughout the entire year—I can well do without eating goose, or any other particular item of food. But, during this festive season, I would never want to miss the enjoyment of the loving company of my wonderful family. With my wife Gussie, my son Kenneth, my daughter-in-law Birte, and my grandchildren Steven, Kevin and Emma, it really becomes *A Very Merry Christmas.*

SHOA DAY IN CANADA

A media report about a statement in our Houses of Parliament had me sufficiently aroused to reveal my concerns to a number of email correspondents. The intended transmission was:

If you recall my "The Nazi Regime" story and other related writings, you know that, as far as I am concerned, Israel as a nation, and Jews as a cultural or a religious group, "can do no wrong". Because of my shared "community guilt"—albeit as an innocent—I reveal my always sympathetic pro-Israel thoughts in relation to Nazis, the Holocaust, and the struggles and sufferings of European Jews in general.

I am presently conducting an "opinion survey" among some of my more knowledgeable friends, and would very much like your perspective—and that of any of your own contacts, if they have strong views on the subject.

According to recent media reports, there has been a unanimous agreement among all parties in our Canadian parliament, to make one day a year a Day of Commemoration of the Shoa.

I don't have to clarify where my sympathies have always been; you could not wish for a more enthusiastic Zionist. Yet, should there really be a Canadian Day of Remembrance for just one of the evils in the world—although certainly one of the major ones?

Once proposed by any person in the House in Ottawa, I can appreciate that none of the parties' representatives would want to disagree. Being affiliated with a constantly "whoring-for-votes" community so prevalent among elected officials, they would fear any loss of a Jewish vote—is there such a thing?—if they objected.

I would have no problem with the commemoration of VE-Day or anything else as a "Freedom from Tyranny" anniversary. We could even have—more appropriately named, of course—something like an "Ethnic Cleansing is Evil" remembrance in Canada. This would, in addition to the Holocaust, recall all the genocides in the world—including such happenings as the Turkish slaughter of the Armenians; the Iraqi subjugation of the Kurds; Stalin's exterminations; the excesses in Rwanda; the treatment of our North American aborigines; or—eh, why not—perhaps even the expulsion of 13 million Germans from Eastern Europe. But making it a Canadian national anniversary, with only the Germans as the baddies, seems a bit much.

Following some reflection I changed my mind. Not about the subject as such, but concerning my intended survey. With this issue, generating so much passion that often displaces reason, the safe course seemed to be to leave any debate to people without my personal connection—however tentative—to make the point. My motives could easily have been misinterpreted. Instead of appearing fair and noble and concerned, I might have come across as an overly sensitive "bloody Kraut".

The Act was "assented to by Parliament" on November 7, 2003, with the date to be determined each year by the Jewish lunar calendar as *Yom ha-Shoa* or Holocaust Memorial Day.

Since that time I had discovered no further coverage by our media. I assumed, therefore, that—like so many items that our elected representatives initially approach with great enthusiasm—it had just quietly gone away.

Not at all, as my search of the internet revealed. On April 20, 2004, some statements by members did indeed introduce the topic in our Parliament, and were recorded by *Hansard* from the House of Commons debate. I wonder if the *Honourable Members* who spoke were aware that this just happened to be the 115th birthday of the primary nemesis, the one who had decreed the holocaust.

THE SHIA–MICK EXCHANGE

Despite a Roman Catholic upbringing, I can hardly qualify for the slightly derogatory term "Mick", since there are absolutely no known Irish in my ancestry. Culturally I could best describe myself as a "lapsed Judeo-Christian"; while religiously, I am a professed atheist—although history of comparative religions has become a favourite topic.

A correspondent, Iraqi by birth, is indeed a Shia Muslim. By heritage, that is, albeit perhaps as lapsed as I am. Even if he has not advanced—or deteriorated—to my current incarnation of total pious incredulity, he might at least meet the criteria of an agnostic. I neither know nor care, and would never ask. However, a lack of *total* commitment to the obligations of his faith might well have been demonstrated at a recent meeting. Although it was during the daylight hours of decreed fasting for Ramadan, he also enjoyed his breakfast. Just as I, with my Catholic upbringing, eat meat most Fridays, despite my ancestral religion's objections.

Our first exchange had been around the time of the Americans' invasion of Iraq in their search for alleged WMDs, or what, in promptly updated Latin, the Vatican described as *universalis destructionis armamenta* (weapons of mass destruction). Following a number of brief chats about the situation, when we met in our professional relationship, I proffered the transmission of some of my pertinent articles. They were not vehemently declined, brought interesting responses, and developed into an almost weekly email interchange of great interest—to me, anyway.

Any type of controversially diverging discussion is rarely resolved, since opposing parties are often deeply committed to their own views and usually—on both sides of the argument—lack all the facts and detailed knowledge to make a serious, educated and well-informed assessment or decision. We are all subject to our own experiences, prejudices and beliefs, frequently based on misinformation. I freely admit that I am probably no exception.

Nevertheless, I found it both interesting and disquieting, how someone at his intellectual level could be "so wrong" on an issue. Conceivably he feels exactly that way about the peculiar opinions, which I unashamedly express. Particularly in my unquestioning support for Zionism, Israel, and the plight of Jews in general; and my identification of Islamist fundamentalist fanatics as the only brand of terrorists that endanger me personally.

We agreed that the invasion of his native land Iraq was, at best, a dubious decision. Yet he felt strongly that the removal of the country's leadership was a commendable effort; whereas I still suspect that Saddam Hussein, while in power, was less of a problem for us *in the Western world* than the current quagmire. Of course, every single one of his Kurdish and Shia countrymen, along with the residents of the neighbouring nations that he attacked, would certainly reject my navel-gazing "Western" views.

We concurred—as it now seems obvious—that while the war effort was clearly identified by the invaders, plans for ensuring the peace were non-existent. He still expresses hope that the country will evolve into a true democracy—something that I find difficult to perceive for *any* Muslim nation. My forecast is still for either a civil war that will result in three jurisdictions for Kurds, Shiite and Sunnis respectively; or a Taliban-type radical government run by religious fanatics. And do I ever hope that I am wrong!

As a resident in today's Iraq, I would be cautious about voicing an opinion condemning the previous rulers of the Baath party; or praising the Western "liberators". With the arrival of a growing number of body bags in the USA, I still fear that the Yanks might just "pack it up" some day, to leave the Iraqis to fend for themselves—by killing each other, of course, the world-wide practice during such conflicts since the beginning of time.

The Americans' ever-lasting staying power in the countries they defeated during World War Two cannot be the benchmark for Iraq since, once they occupied Germany and Japan, that war was over. The death of occupiers was more likely the result of traffic accidents and never caused by local insurgents.

We had an interesting exchange following my contact's return from a recent family visit to Iraq. Among other eyewitness reports he observed the lack of border control that allows anyone to enter. In the views of many of his former countrymen, the situation is encouraged by the Americans. It facilitates access to this combat zone by extremists of any ilk, and thereby allows the Western occupiers to fight such fanatics in faraway places rather than in the USA. Why not, eh?

Since then he and I found ourselves in total agreement when recognizing the antagonism of all their neighbouring countries to a democratic Iraq. Obviously, if this US-instigated "liberation Iraq" escapade should eventually prove successful, it would be a threatening portent for all the despotic patriarchal, dictatorial or fundamentalist administrations in the area. Surely even Israel prefers a fratricidal conflict among Arab neighbours to any strongly united Muslim nation—democratic or otherwise.

The greatest divergence in our views remains on the Palestinian question. My approach to this subject is forever emotional and often illogical. For the—to me they are—most compelling reasons I outlined in earlier writings, my sympathies have always been on the side of the Israelis. Yet even when I try to look at this objectively—with my prejudices this is not an easy task, so I admit—I cannot get away from certain basics.

The State of Israel is surrounded by countries of Muslim Arabs who actively strive to destroy the Jewish nation, or at least would not object if this was done by the fanatics in their midst. Squalid conditions and the radical Islamist teachings in the refugee camps, where Palestinians have been "warehoused" for over fifty years, are a breeding ground for terrorists who have nothing to lose in this world and everything to gain in paradise by blowing themselves up. Of course, whether they can be rewarded with *virgins* or with *raisins*, once they perish through self-immolation, remains unclear. Some scholars interpreting the Prophet's alleged revelations from *Allah* disagree on what awaits these suicidal murderers.

Quite naively, I must admit, I relate the Palestinians' situation to the expulsion of ethnic Germans from what later—at least politically—became known as Eastern Europe. These German refugees were, albeit grudgingly, accepted and eventually fully integrated into the Western part of Europe.

Of course, it was Germans as a belligerent nation who, as the original perpetrators, provoked such retribution; while Palestinians were the innocent sufferers. These Arabs had the Jews of a war-torn world bestowed on them by the decrees of mainly European co-conspirators. Israel's 1948 *War of Independence* truly became the Palestinians' *al-Nakba* (catastrophe). Yet once ethnically cleansed from their homeland, both Germans and Arabs were initially in the same unfortunate situation. The Germans made the resettlement a success; the Arabs still endure theirs as a continuing tragedy.

My friend might well feel that, from a Muslim-Arab perspective, the unfortunate ethnic Germans of that turmoil—my wife is one of them—should *never* have been accepted nor fully integrated by the surrounding countries. Their assimilation could be perceived as a shamefully dishonouring concession made to the occupying enemy, both by those displaced and by their reluctantly welcoming ethnic brethren. Instead these German refugees should perhaps have been settled in camps, awaiting their eventual return. This could have implanted in them, too, nothing but ever-lasting hatred for the opposing Poles, the Russians, and the nationals of the Balkan states, who now possessed their homes and properties. What a dismal situation that would be!

His former countrymen considered the law, barring Palestinians from integration into Iraq, one of a previous government's wiser decrees. They assess similar rejection of the dispossessed by other nations in the Middle East as equally commendable. The aim of such tragic action was, of course, that the "right to return" could continue as the first priority in the minds of doomed refugees; within their unsympathetic or otherwise scheming neighbour states; and among bleeding-heart communities around the world.

What Israeli government would so recklessly consent to such a resettlement? Does any reasonably pragmatic Arab, who has not been swayed by his religious teachings, or can anticipate nothing but a desolate life in a refugee camp, *really* consider this as a possibility? For me, having Israeli Jews as a minority, and Palestinian Arabs as the overwhelming majority, "share" a united Palestine, is a fantasy. But my correspondent considers it a basic prerequisite for a final resolve.

Where we can agree, again, is that Western media—especially in the USA—usually support the Israelis; just as I do myself. We are also in accord that, without the financial contributions from the world's Jewry, and the assistance from sympathizing governments of the West, primarily the USA, Israel might not have survived amid a sea of antagonistic neighbours.

As a youth he had experienced the political indoctrination by the Baathist dictatorship, just as I encountered it from the Nazis in Germany. Both of us, no doubt because of our home environment, did not succumb. Similar attempted recruitment of the young goes on today, even in Canada where—in my opinion, which he does not share—some Canadian-born descendants of Muslim and Jewish immigrants are brainwashed by religious teachings in their respective *Madressas* and *Yeshivas*. Vigorous promotion of hatred among their respective adherents creates ever more fanatics to endorse their causes.

He views Islam as a peaceful faith. My readings in history have candidly revealed much brutal violence "in the name of religion". The origin of Islam, and its later extension into Northern Africa and Spain, I have seen reported as rather blood-soaked events. This horror might, of course, have been surpassed by the preceding terror, which Christians created or experienced, as they expanded their own religion around the world; or later when they competed with each other since the Reformation.

My contact questions why I view everything from a *Canadian* perspective. No doubt he means that I reflect the prevalent navel-gazing approach to world events, so naively contemplated by many of us on both sides of the border in

North America. Of course, as a Canadian—particularly as a citizen of this fortunate country *by choice*—how else would I want to see the universe?

Before I commit myself to save the world, I want to ensure a continuation of my own life in the environment that I thoroughly appreciate. Danger to me and my countrymen—as I see it—comes only from Islamist fundamentalists. I need not fear the fanatic extremists among Israeli settlers; Basques; Punjabis; Tamils; Tutsis; or the few remaining irreconcilable Irish; even if they fight constantly with their real or perceived enemies. While I might get hurt as a mere "innocent bystander" at one of their target sites—even in down-town Toronto during a shoot-out by rival criminal gangs—I would have the, albeit unhelpful, solace that I was not the *intended* target. It is only the self-immolating lunatics among Islamists that, for their kamikaze-type attacks, consider me and "my kind"—which is really anyone with a Western orientation, including liberal-thinking Muslims—as an enemy. No other ethnic or religious groups' maniacs seem to take special pride in such imbecilic warfare directed at me personally.

I would have no serious concerns about conflicts abroad, if the combatants could just kill each other and leave me and my Canadian countrymen out of their struggle. Even if—unimaginable!—Germans and Poles, or Germans and French, who, until I left there, had always been deadly enemies and today "occupy" each others' ancient lands, were still slaughtering each other. If they proceeded on their own turf, it would hopefully not involve me as a Canadian.

I agree with my correspondent that it is often poverty and the hopelessness of their lot that breeds ever more radicals among the young. Yet those from India or China or Africa are no threat to me—not yet, anyway, unless they converted to Islam. And unquestionably it is the corrupt authoritarian rulers in countries with masses of "the great unwashed" that keep these unfortunates exploited. The wealth of oil-rich states in the Middle East could surely have solved the misery of all Palestinians long ago—had there been the political will to do this.

But then, as a Canadian, how dare I criticize foreigners about the plight of their underprivileged. What am I doing to solve the problems of the disadvantaged in my own country? Perhaps as much as a third of Canada's aboriginal population still remains stored on reservations. These, our very own "refugees from civilization"—albeit by their own choice and, perplexingly, with my government's encouragement and enormous financial support—have been similarly vegetating over two centuries.

This lets me add another *mea culpa* to the community guilt that—with my ethnic background—I already bear because of the holocaust. Although I am personally equally innocent, I could also carry the guilt for the misdeeds of my fellow-Europeans in their subjugation of the American Indians.

Yet I suffer no such painful qualms about the historically created mess in the Middle East. I felt much more secure as a leave-me-alone Canadian while there was a Communist regime in Afghanistan; Iran existed under the Shah; and Saddam Hussein was the dictator in Iraq; than I do with the present mayhem in all three countries. Although I recognize that, in these jurisdictions, the purging of perceived "undesirables" by previous regimes was horrifyingly lethal for the local victims.

One must have misgivings about the Machiavellian betrayal by the French and English, even the Italians—and on the fringes the Americans as well—almost a hundred years ago; and the scheming by Ibn Saud and Shareef Husain and other local chieftains of their time; all as co-conspirators. Yet I feel no responsibility for these injustices, or for the enduring poverty in the area. Some of the oil-producing countries have a higher per-capita-income than even Canada. Should I be blamed for the thousands of degenerate local princelings and corrupt political leaders, who are the only beneficiaries of the immense wealth in their part of the world?

After months of frequent interchange, my regular pen-pal—now, so I dare hope, an evolving friend—and I had to concur, that there are controversies in the international field on which we agree to disagree. With some of our more recent emails we strayed onto much less divisive subjects, when we exchanged ideas on gardening, investments, or our local politics. Yet, even with relatively "harmless" topics, one can still differ occasionally. This, of course, is the Canadian way; it makes the interchange interesting and—hopefully—enduring.

My correspondent is familiar with all my writings, including the minute details of this chapter. Yet he would never agree to become the publicly revealed "source" for his observations. Had we communicated, with me in the capacity of a journalist—which I do not (yet?) profess to be—his pronouncements would all have been "off the record". And even torture—or a Supreme Court ruling—could not make me disclose my sources!

SARS in Toronto

SARS had quickly turned into the globally recognized and widely feared acronym for *severe acute respiratory syndrome.* Early in 2003, it became of great concern in our immediate area as well. Suddenly, international travel was something to be avoided.

Arrangements for my own journey to my annual high school reunion in Germany had already been made. What to do? Pertinent extract quotes from the email correspondence that I personally composed and sent to one of my friends, the organizer of this *Klassentreffen,* describes it all. It is translated from my original German.

April 25, 2003:

Perhaps I should cancel my participation for May 16th? I certainly do not want to impose on my dear friends, and create anxieties because of their fear of a possible infection.

The current international media reports (they seem to put us in the same category as China) must surely create considerable apprehension for some classmates.

Here is the real story, as I read it: The Chinese kept their problem a secret, or at least minimized the extent of the outbreak. An old lady, who recently returned from a visit to her native soil, had been contaminated while in China. Without anyone's knowledge she infected her immediate family in Toronto, then the members of her church congregation, and eventually the staff of the hospital where she had been admitted with a suspected "ordinary" pneumonia. All her contact persons were quarantined; sixteen died; more than half of the others have already been discharged; some 200 to 300, who were in contact with these people, are still in quarantine.

All this occurred in the eastern part of Toronto. We ourselves live in Mississauga, to the west; have not visited downtown Toronto for two months; or the eastern part of the city in several years. But—just the same!

The political opportunists at the World Health Organization, to satisfy the Chinese, must, of course, take drastic action against us as well; as they would have against the USA or any other "Western" nation. The result is that they warn the world against visits to Toronto.

April 26, 2003:

Our politicians and the entire business community are most concerned about the WHO's travel advisory. Although it seems that the local situation is well in hand.

I appreciate your positive response. However, I would not want any of our friends, still uneasy about this situation—in order to spare my feelings—have to state other reasons to justify their cancellation.

I cannot expect that the WHO in Geneva will cancel their travel warning as early as next week. They could never admit now that, with their "do not travel to Toronto" edict, they were much too hasty.

Unlike with the WHO, to be *politically correct* is not the major priority of the Center for Disease Control in Atlanta/USA. Therefore I have much more confidence in their revelations. Their only recommendation is that, while in Toronto, one should avoid visits to hospitals.

The approximately 100 persons still remaining in healthcare facilities have been there since the original outbreak. Everyone who had contact with these continues in "voluntary quarantine" (remains at home for two weeks), to avoid a possible further spread of contamination, should they indeed have themselves been infected. Symptoms are high fever, dry cough and severe head aches.

Authorities in Denmark, as we just discovered while expecting a guest, do not convey concern to their citizens who plan to visit here. And, I reiterate, we do not live in Toronto and have not visited there since the initial outbreak.

April 27, 2003:

The decision has been made. I do fly to Stuttgart for a visit with our friends. They commented that, a single drive on the autobahn from Stuttgart to Karlsruhe might be more dangerous than the possibility of catching SARS from such a cautious resident of Mississauga, as I am.

However, if any of our classmates are still concerned, I will avoid this year's reunion and spend the extra day in Stuttgart.

April 30, 2003:

The Canadian delegation, which met with WHO management in Geneva yesterday, was assured that the travel warning for Toronto would be officially rescinded today.

Our banishment was of great interest to the international media. The termination of it, however, will make no headlines outside our immediate area. The primary concern is now to re-invigorate our tourism industry. This started last night when, for a sporting event, the remaining unsold tickets went for $1 each, which ensured a full house of 50,000 attendees.

Later on April 30, 2003:

The SARS Travel warning for Toronto has been officially cancelled. That should reassure all possible participants for our reunion about my being "free of contamination".

Obviously we cannot expect official apologies from the WHO, because of their hasty panic-creating declaration the previous week. That they did enormous damage to our tourism industry will hardly concern their bureaucracy.

The media-alleged admission of the head of this UN-affiliate was simply that, because there were so many inquiries on the subject, experts felt that Toronto should be branded as "diseased" for a 21-day period, by which time one expected to have "things sorted out". Such irresponsible action can certainly not be revealed in their public commentary. And for the international press, the "all clear for Toronto" is no longer a worthy story for coverage.

During May 2003, I did indeed go for my annual visit and enjoyed myself as usual. None of my classmates seemed to recoil from me when I approached to give them my usual hug.

CHARITIES

My father made it a maxim following a World War One experience. "Do not volunteer for anything" was the advice he gave me, his only son. His personal recollection from the military was that, following a show of hands from the musically talented, when asked if they knew how to play the piano, those so identified quickly transferred to kitchen duty for the peeling of spuds.

Many of my former colleagues, some personal friends and also several neighbours, enthusiastically devote many hours of their time to—what they must surely consider, and perhaps these really are—"worthy" causes. They seem to enjoy their assignments, which range from eldercare; hospital assistance; patient transportation; delivery of meals-on-wheels; assignments at food banks; the construction of living quarters for the needy; and over a variety of many others; right to door-to-door canvassing for various charitable causes.

Our significantly disadvantaged may indeed need society's assistance. We did not all start out with loving and supportive parents. And for reasons of health, infirmity or old age, some of our fellow-citizens may unquestionably be incapable of coping with all of life's demands that are placed on them. If they do not have family members who can help, there is justification for other assistance. The problem that I see is with the inefficient way in which such aid is provided.

My first choice in most spheres has always been for the government to "stay out of my face", whenever the private sector could fill a need or a demand. However, I hold the opposite view where this applies to the provision of services for the underprivileged. My preference would be to rather pay an extra thousand dollars in taxes, before I happily contribute even as little as a hundred bucks to a charitable cause.

I see it as the government's role to grant the *really* needy (note the *italics*) the necessities of life. Where such support is not provided, our efforts as responsible citizens should be towards the persuasion of our officialdom, to remedy the situation; rather than setting up a multitude of programs through overlapping charitable organizations.

Currently I observe that, where the authorities are already involved and do hand out my tax money, this is often done wastefully. Yet again, where the government serves a client group ineffectively, we should desist from giving up and taking over. We could instead convincingly protest through our political representatives and intensify our insistence on better services.

Instead of what I would consider an orderly routine, we have thousands—according to the Canadian Centre for Philanthropy, there are 74,918 (seventy-four *thousand*!) registered in Canada right now—groups of do-gooders who trip over each other in bothering me and my fellow citizens for contributions in time or money. I also read recently that the administration charges of a $20 contribution in a door-to-door canvass may well exceed the value of the gifted amount.

I would be quite interested in the real cost to taxpayers of some of the charitable events. Those cycling, marching, jumping, running, swimming—even *eating*—for supposedly worthy causes often create traffic chaos and usually require police escorts, security barriers, clean-up crews and—after the participants overexerted or over-indulged themselves—perhaps medical care. The donations which they procure also result in reduced taxes on earnings or profits for the contributors.

Some of these events are sponsored by religious or service groups. Others derive their initial support from business affiliations. Whenever participation in a cause is decreed under such an umbrella sponsorship, the actual helpers assigned might be drafted by their organizations rather than volunteer on their own.

In a working environment, it is indeed advisable to eagerly accept suggestions for the donation of time and money—at least one should display such enthusiasm on the outside. The true feelings about the merit of the cause and the intrusion on one's own leisure and finances—for occasionally rather dubious projects—might best be kept a secret.

Membership in church or service groups has never aroused my interest. This spared me from such tasks, which might have impressed my fellow-parishioners or association members. During my career I have usually been fortunate—from my atrociously biased perspective, of course—by not ending up with such assignments; or where put onto me, I was able to "delegate" to someone more deserving of the honours.

Many of the keenly interested surely do this from their real commitment to a cause. It falls into their perception of the "I'm my brothers' keeper" universe. Some others, as mere eager-beavers, might make the sacrifice to help advance their careers. And a few, so I suspect, will partake to spice up their social engagements, with at least a part of their expenses being reimbursed or becoming tax deductible.

Those chosen for lengthy projects by their organizations' management—from several of my observations—often meet certain criteria. On the positive side they are at least reasonably intelligent for the task at hand. After all, their parent organization does not want to be embarrassed when delegating some dunce. The drafted volunteers are also sufficiently articulate—or at least gabby—and, for the more senior tasks, they usually have sufficient organizational strengths or qualify as "sales-types". Yet, in my cynical assessment, I often experienced those awarded with any long-term assignments to be typical of the not-really-missed representatives in their actual work environment. Otherwise, how could they be delegated to such stints for a period of weeks or even months?

With this statement I will most certainly offend more people than I can amuse. I might even lose some friends whose feelings I have hurt. But again, let me reiterate, any *real* friends of mine—in this line of endeavour—will always have been among those who volunteered from conviction, and not ever because their management made them the sacrificial lamb and didn't mind to "get this guy out of here for a while".

Whoever comes to our door for solicitation—or the promotion of commercial products or services, for that matter—I usually approach with my friendliest demeanour and the statement "Whatever you are selling, we have two of them already and never use either one". Once a few enlighten me that they do not want me to buy, but are merely doing their good deed, I might add "While I recognize yours as a worthy cause, I focus my donations exclusively on a small number of charities and, unfortunately, yours isn't one of them". That takes care of all the strangers. Others, however, such as neighbours or, worse still, their kids, I accommodate with some of my money; and even these—in my opinion—"useless" contributions can amount to a few hundred dollars a year.

My latest immediate response to those soliciting by telephone could well be "Which jail are you calling from?" Recent media reports suggested that some telemarketing is done by inmates from our penal institutions.

There are, indeed, a few organizations, to which I regularly donate what I consider to be substantial amounts. For these I always insist on *not* being listed as one of their donors. Yet, even for my favourites among the causes that I support with charitable donations, I cannot help thinking that "I've just been had", when I pay. After all, medical care—one of my beneficiaries—along with education and the basic-living support for the needy, rank very much at the top of my list of services that should be generally and "freely" available to all—from taxes, of course.

Extending charitable assistance to a level prescribed by some religions has never stirred my enthusiasm. Abandoning still more of my worldly possessions would not really make our planet a better place. The lot of the underprivileged would not improve either, if, after sharing all my wealth with them, I would become one of their number. Even—what to some is—a paltry tithing, I would consider as excessive; and I do admit this without embarrassment.

But then, with my strong views that the needy should be supported from taxes, I am already a significant contributor. Considering the basic assessment; the government's claw-back of Old Age Security; and the elimination of the Age Deduction for seniors in my range; my marginal tax rate is a significant part of my income. Who can expect me to do even more?

When our son went to school, one regularly forced him into collection assignments. We did not want him to go "begging" from friends or neighbours, and, therefore, usually paid ourselves, just enough to satisfy his cause without having to elicit contributions from others.

Merely to get to know the neighbourhood, Ken did not have to go pleading for support in our area. He had his door-to-door introduction through the entrepreneurial system, when he delivered catalogues to earn his pocket money since the age of eight. Nor would he have been able to detect the generous or stingy characteristics of our fellow citizens. A friend, who persistently tithes in excess—he does not just talk about it, he *really* gives more than ten percent of his income—extends all this generosity to one and only one association. He turns down requests from everyone else, who probably consider him miserly.

The *exploitation* of the young—in my terminology and assessment, not that of most people—still goes on. Perhaps it is just intended as their training for many future assignments as volunteers for *worthy* causes. I observe that my grandchildren, as well, often passionately approach the task of raising money for one cause or other. On a number of occasions—when I was personally drafted as one of their contributors—I noticed that their parents, too, had kept them from *yet again* canvassing their district, by limiting our kids' relatively "sizeable" collections to what they could raise from within the family.

Statistics on these matters appear well hidden or—like most data—are merely interpreted to confirm a preconceived bias. I gathered none to make my point. The "horror stories" that I encountered were mainly anecdotal. But I do have some very personal experiences with people who abused the system.

An overwhelming problem manifests itself by the apparent lack of any useful coordination between the well-meaning support groups. Even if this was desired, with the immense number of charities it might not really be practical or effective.

Those who know the routine can get handouts from many sources. What annoyed me the most was their eventual bragging—to me for one—about the inanity of the system; and the naive individual contributors, whom they considered to be real "suckers". I would hope that these exploiters are the exception rather than the norm; but they are really the only ones that have come to my personal attention.

Recent reports—again mainly anecdotal—allege the forceful demands on their ethnic brethren by various terrorist groups, for financial contributions to "the struggle in the homeland". These disgusting activities on our soil should be stopped immediately! But only since 9/11 do our governments and media dare to even mention their existence in the Western world.

Yet, the bleeding-heart component of our society immediately categorizes my views and those of others like me as discrimination or police-state tactics. My allegedly *heartless* attitude towards charitable support for the reportedly disadvantaged can be easily branded as extreme. So call me a "*redneck*" if you like. See if I care!

EXPLOITING THE SYSTEM

Some of my fellow-citizens waste my tax dollars on frivolous acquisitions, through casual neglect and by wicked if not illicit abuse of the services provided by all levels of our governments. And no one in authority seems to want to address the issue. Is it from fear of a voter backlash?

Where is a Mike-Harris-type of government when we need it? As Premier of Ontario he did indeed take decisive and unwavering action consistent with his promises in two election crusades. During his second term in office, following the resentment created by bleeding-heart liberals; special interest groups; "the great unwashed"; and the relentless promotion of their gripes by much of the media; he became totally *unelectable.*

When he resigned as leader, he was replaced by a wishy-washy candidate from within his own cabinet, whom the party's gurus perceived as an appropriate vote-catching persuader of the masses. Yet, resulting in part from the even more convincing lies proffered by the opposition party during the campaign, he lost the next election just the same. And he deserved this rejection!

There must be hundreds of useless activities which, with a serious commitment by our current "political *leaders*"—isn't this term an oxymoron in itself?—could be eliminated. Much abuse of the system by an equally scheming electorate—they are learning from their governing overlords—could at least be curtailed.

Always as my favourite target remains the lavish support of multiculturalism. It provides operational funds for scores of "executives" and staff from ethnic, religious and racial organizations, who then waste my tax dollars to encourage the retention of their groups' dissimilarities—rather than to have them integrated into Canada's traditional way of life.

Wastage that impacts on our environment is another one of my occasional grumbles. As but one example, it is the resistance to recycle effectively, which results in more garbage than necessary. To avoid payment of the *at long last* established fees for the weekly removal of more than three garbage bags per household, some homeowners now practise various ingenious schemes. The ultimate in gall is when these offenders deposit their excess garbage into the collection bins in parks or public buildings; or discard their old car batteries and tires along isolated roadsides.

It is easy to detect that the overload of the healthcare system is augmented by hypochondriacs. Waiting rooms in doctors' offices and the emergency departments in hospitals have their assembly of fantasizing patients, who insist on consultations with professionals for even the most insignificant of exaggerated or totally imaginary ailments.

This is all for free, of course, so they reason. Where do they think the money comes from? Surely, if assessed a minimum charge for each session, many could be discouraged from appearing as often.

Yet patients are only partially at fault. I also blame those medical caregivers, who seem to encourage repeat visits and excessively refer their regular clientele for further examinations to specialists and for elaborate tests in laboratories. Why, I wonder; might it be to protect themselves against a Southern-US-type of jury award because of neglect, should they ever be accused of misdiagnosis? Is there safety in a larger number of defendants, when charged with erroneous analysis? Or is their objective to create more profitable traffic for their doctor-friends or for the medical centres which they partially own?

Repeat consultations for many of these abusing patients, each one financed in total by a government health plan, increase the cost to me as a taxpayer. It has been suggested that our Provincial Plan, OHIP, would unquestioningly pay the visits for even minor concerns to as many as five doctors within one week; just as long as the patient does not contact two different physicians on the very same day, since only this might alert the system. Yet even then, if the alleged problem is described or assessed in another way, the same-day visits would both be covered as well.

It seems scandalous to me that such misuse is not eliminated. Surely a patient's registration with one doctor—and only with one—as his or her "very own" general practitioner should be promoted; and overuse then further discouraged with a basic fee for each consultation payable by the apparent sufferer. There should also be a constant assessment of the appropriateness of referrals that physicians initiate.

Health care might well be the costliest visible item on a provincial budget; but even more money seems to be lost to government coffers by the underground economy. "Will you pay cash for this" is a question commonly asked by tradesmen before they quote a price.

With this scheme, if successful, the least one "saves" from the bill—at current provincial and federal sales tax rates—is a 15% surcharge. However, since the contractor then does not declare his income from the project, he is not taxed at all and—here they penalize me again—my share of general taxes must become correspondingly higher.

There are tax benefits to operating a small business. Surely the owners find ways to claim many of their personal "operating expenses" for telephones, rent, lighting and heating, car leasing, even cleaning and gardening at their homes. And in major organizations the expense-account meal and entertainment abuse seems customary, as is a general waste in government and private sector bureaucracies.

I must admit that—since I cannot partake—I am somewhat resentful of the questionable deductions successfully justified by small entrepreneurs; and the lavish entertainment and excessively generous benefits enjoyed in some of the big concerns. Of course, with the circumvention of sales tax through "cash purchases", I, too, would prefer to become one of the offending parties. So seems to be just about everyone with whom I reviewed this subject.

You would be perceived a liar or a fool, were you to deny that you do not at least envy those who successfully scheme to benefit from such tax-avoidance practices. Therefore, guilty as I am of aspiring—even if not succeeding—perhaps I should not complain as zealously?

FRUGAL VERSUS CHEAP

Spendthrift and wasteful I never was. Frugal—but not cheap—is the term I would favour to describe my behaviour. At least, this is how I always saw myself. None of my friends ever mentioned anything to the contrary. If they observed an aberration in me, they would surely have let me know, and I could have mended my ways.

Yet I occasionally detect such shortcomings in others. They probably do not recognize their atypical habits as peculiar. Otherwise, why would they continue with such idiosyncrasies?

An acquaintance—whom I consider to be quite wealthy—would split a cent, if possible, when determining how to share the bill among diners. A fifteen per-cent gratuity is also considered excessive during this transaction, even if based merely on the net amount of the bill, excluding the taxes. The remaining buns served with the meal are always collected, while emphasizing that "we have paid for them".

Still more extreme is what I occasionally observed from others. I am happy to state that these people were total strangers. While feeling themselves unobserved, they stocked up on sugar bags and the tiny cream containers from the bowls on their tables. Really!

Under the right circumstances, bringing home the meat component of a meal that cannot be fully consumed in a restaurant is what I consider as frugal. While the frequently used terminology for the packaging is still *doggie bag*, one no longer needs to camouflage this reclamation of a left-over as being "for my dog".

I would only consider such a request while eating in a *family-type* establish-ment, with members of my immediate family or among close friends. In larger groups, or while dining with mere acquaintances, I would decline. Of course, the stocking up by anyone with food items from a self-serve buffet, I would always judge as being disgustingly cheap.

Seniors' discounts in stores, theatres and restaurants are meant for those over 65. I occasionally witness the abuse of this benefit. While notices prominently displayed indicate that verification of dubious claimants might be required, the servers are usually too polite—or embarrassed—to insist on this proof-of-age.

The ultimate in gall, if demanding such discounts, is when, as the host to obviously "youngish" invited guests, one claims the reduction for the entire party of *alleged* seniors. This, too, I have observed on occasion.

Many people are quite finicky when they determine how much to tip. In this category I have merely heard about this one aberration, with the name of the offending acquaintance mentioned; although I never witnessed his revolting conduct myself. The appalling comment by this real cheapskate was that "I will never come here again, so why should I leave *any* tip". Doesn't this frequent world traveler, who is remarkably wealthy by inheritance rather than through his own initiative, realize that he deprives the employees in the service industry of their just entitlements?

On rare occasions I notice that a beverage, an appetizer or a dessert have been omitted from my restaurant bill. I unfailingly point this out to my attendant. The usual response is a "never mind"—no doubt to avoid awareness by management that such a blunder, favouring the customer, has been made by the employee. Whenever the original invoice was not amended, I used to add an equivalent amount to the gratuity. Only recently did it occur to me that I should change this routine, since it rewarded inefficiency, and the server's dishonesty towards the company.

One chap I know has the widely circulated reputation of being miserly. To me he boasted about his inexpensive haircuts—they looked like it, too, so I noticed. What I found astonishing, however, was his justification for not leaving a gratuity. Since his barber is also the owner of the establishment, so he reasons, he might become offended, since tips are only for "the hired help". Am I incorrect in considering this as merely his poor excuse for being stingy?

Of course, I might arouse similar suspicions with the manner in which I ask my hair to be treated—what little remains of it. The cut I receive from my barber is short enough to provide me with a totally wind-resistant coiffure that, at times, endures for ten weeks before the next trimming is required. Yet I merely consider this a practical arrangement, and never thought of the monetary implications. Honestly!

Most people happily accept repeated invitations to be wined and dined in the homes of others. Fortunately there are only very few of these who would never think of responding in kind. Of course, they quickly get to be notorious and find themselves off the list of invitees.

For us this hasn't been a challenge in recent years, ever since we, ourselves, discontinued such entertainment altogether. Our diminishing number of surviving friends similarly curtailed their instigation of social gatherings. In their case, as in ours, this did not relate to a financial burden; but hosting anyone in our home for what used to be the customary sit-down dinner—at our current age—has just become "too much bloody work and commotion".

During my business travels I encountered what I considered as the ultimate in penny-pinching. The company policy was to reimburse washing and cleaning costs during trips exceeding seven days. One chap—fortunately he wasn't allowed to travel too often—really exploited this. He would bring along soiled shirts and suits from home, to have them laundered at his hotel as soon as he reached day eight.

A good friend cheerfully describes himself as "cheap" when he explains his routine while visiting movie theatres. Otherwise I know him as a generous and most hospitable person. When he reads this story, he will know that I, too, agree with him that this is his one and only anomaly. To avoid the—admittedly somewhat inflated—prices for snacks and beverages, he brings along his own nourishment.

Popcorn or other noshes I would never buy for myself; and quenching my thirst with water from a drinking fountain, is what I merely consider as both healthier and not being wasteful. But smuggling in any store-bought soft drink or other sustenance is really cheap! I must clarify, however, that—while I attend movie screenings with my grandchildren—the prices at the concession stands are no obstacle for me to finance whatever the little darlings desire.

While on my favourite topic, my beloved grandchildren, I can state categorically and with great satisfaction that neither of our off-spring will ever be cheap. Like their parents, they are often generous in the extreme. I just wish they could develop a little more frugality. As their mother reassures me, sometimes such talents skip a generation. If they are late developers in this field, they may still surprise this proud grandfather.

THINGS WE EAT

Exploring "new" things has always been one of my many interests. When eating for gustatory pleasure—and not just for the fuel that I ingest as a slightly chubby *nutritional overachiever*—I extend such enthusiastic experiments to my selection of food as well. Something unknown listed on a menu might indeed encourage me to investigate, always in the expectation of another ambrosial delight. Especially during my many years of international travel, I consumed—and most often really enjoyed—a number of items which others might find less than appetizing.

Out of necessity, immediately after the war—hunger removes most barriers—I had frequently eaten horsemeat in Germany; and just because it was part of the local cuisine, much later occasionally in France. I also ingested shark fin soup in Hong Kong; enjoyed dog stew in Korea; endured sheep eyeball in the Middle East; and sampled chocolate-covered ants at some South American (was it Columbian?) function. I also experienced *Sakana No Ikizukuri* in Japan, which they wisely call "living" rather than "dying" fish. The latter would be a more appropriate description, since that is exactly what the suffering creature does in front of your eyes, while you swallow bites from the filets that have been sliced off both sides of its still living frame.

Our cultural hang-ups make food either perfectly appropriate for our own environment, or something disgustingly alien. Yet there are undeniably many strange things—in the eyes of others—which we enjoy in our Western environment as well.

I grew up with an occasional diet of *Sauerkraut* or *Choucroute*—its name depending on the side of the river Rhine, where it was being acquired—often served with pigs' feet. Those without a German or a French background might reject it for being nothing but decomposing cabbage. They could also recoil from devouring the meal's meat component.

Until I emigrated, we lived close to the border with France, which made snails and frog legs an occasional delight. Of course, in later life, I occasionally wondered how many tourists or business travellers eating *escargot* and *grenouilles*, did really know what they were selecting from the menu.

Foie gras remained a delicacy for me, even after I had discovered how the growth of an enlarged goose liver was encouraged. As a young lad, on frequent visits to a farming community, I had watched the force-feeding of the unfortunate critters when, through a metal funnel, the geese had an overabundance of corn stuffed down their gullets.

Brain or pancreas—reportedly of calf—was one of my father's favourites. At times I still sample it where it is offered in reliable restaurants.

How many diners know that *tripe*—I sample this occasionally when travelling in Europe—is really the stomach lining of cattle?

Caviar is considered a delicacy. Its depiction as mere "fish eggs" might ruin some people's appetite, even if they could afford the price.

They are called *prairie oysters*. Under their real name of bull testicles, they might not be so much in demand.

Cheeses of the "runny" type—*Limburger* or the German *Handkäse* are examples—emit a stench similar to that of a rotting carcass during a heat-wave. Yet this is something to enjoy!

Steak Tatar, consisting mainly of raw beef, is not everyone's favourite either.

The Swedes' *Sur Strömning,* or the Norwegians' *Rak Orret* seem unsurpassed as a foul smelling fish delicacy.

Sushi and *Sashimi* have become widely accepted in Western society. I am now somewhat less enthusiastic about eating *any* raw fish, ever since viewing an investigative report on Television. It showed the large number of little worms that crawled out of a filet of raw fish as it was being heated up.

Even the basic foods that we consider as part of our almost daily diet, some other cultures regard with abhorrence. Depending on their religious teachings, beef, pork or shellfish rank a definite dietary no-no in much of the world.

We seem to have no problem while eating "the Easter bunny" or "little Bambi". Even "Rudolph the red-nosed Reindeer" can appear well camouflaged on the menu. Just don't tell your young children what it is that they are being offered at dinner.

The mere sight of a lobster keeps some people from savouring this delight. Many others feel this way about shrimp, octopus and crab legs as well. And one has to be a connoisseur to slurp oysters from the shell.

The name alone can turn many people off eating *Blood Pudding*, which for me is just another kind of sausage. *Head Cheese* falls into this category as well.

And many would feel embarrassed to order something named *Spotted Dick*, unless it is in a restaurant in Britain, where this dessert—I recall it as a kind of bread pudding containing raisins—seems appreciated.

My father was most particular about his food. He had always enjoyed chicken. This ended right after his visit to a farmyard, where he noticed one of the little beasts searching for nourishment in a recently dropped horse apple. That banned any kind of fowl from his list of nourishments.

Rather late in life—during a visit in Canada—he accompanied a friend for his first-ever fishing trip. That took another product off his menu. Until then he had not realized that worms were the preferred bait used by the anglers of that time, and therefore, so he just discovered, obviously part of the regular diet of a fish.

Despite their description, he had no trouble eating *Spätzle* or "little sparrows", a harmless local pasta where I grew up. The regional dialect in Northern Baden had many peculiarly named dishes. *Bubespitzle*, which translates as "little boy's penis", was a potato-flour concoction and one of our many frequent meals. And *Nonnenfürzle* or "Nun's little farts", one could enjoy as an after-dinner sweet.

As it applies to culinary delights, I am very glad that I did not take after my parents, especially my father, who was not at all adventurous in his sampling of unknown food. I would have missed out on many really delightful experiences.

Sex as a Theme

This should be the shortest of all my recordings. If, intrigued by the title, anyone particularly inquisitive has already skipped to this chapter—expecting juicy details of my life experiences—he or she will be sorely disappointed.

One enraptured reader of my earlier books had deplored the lack of erotic revelations. I was raised in a culture, where the adage "*Ein Kavalier geniesst und schweigt*" (A *real* gentleman enjoys *discreetly*) was taken seriously—at least by me. Not that anyone should read into these comments that I would have actual secrets to reveal!

Heterosexual encounters were often the bragged-about topics of my contemporaries. I would suspect that more lies than truths were reported by many of the wishful great lovers, if they were men; or by their at least in the females' own imagination—allegedly widely desired potential counterparts. With those talking the most no doubt experiencing the least of such delights.

The youths of today, if they are abstainers, may still resort to cold showers and other home remedies, in lieu of the real thing. As practitioners, however, they are reportedly much more relaxed about the issue. You aim; you score; it is no big deal. So there is no need to prevaricate or even talk about it at all. This seems to be their approach.

In my generation, where it applied to homosexual experiences during childhood, these remained as well-camouflaged incidents. Such experiments of the "perverse kind" were a subject that was totally taboo. Only in recent years, as ever more of the formerly violated youngsters dare to speak up, does one talk about this publicly. Revelations by some victims then encourage others to come forward with reports about their own encounters. If there are financial benefits to be pressured out of the real or alleged abusers, or the equally denounced wealthy organizations they represented, not necessarily truthful violations may be reported as well.

An acquaintance, whose entire schooling was in another country, appears amused and wonders why there would now be such an outrage. In his words, "If you attended an independent school, were a member of a youth organization, or served as one of the priests' little helpers, there was always someone with his hands inside your trousers". I failed completely to see any humour in this reaction to child-molestation. Perhaps it was the Nazis' much publicized "final solution", also applied to pedophiles, which, during my childhood, shielded me from such encounters.

As teenagers, girls of my generation were worried about getting pregnant, while the boys' only trepidation concerned catching VD. So, while sex might have been foremost on our minds, one tried to curtail one's explorations—quite often unsuccessfully, I must admit.

After the release of the pill during the free-living sixties, when "If it feels good, do it" became the axiom, many people who had advanced to my age group were either too busy making a living, or had religious, moral or family concerns, which made them hesitate to get involved. At least, if they were sufficiently adventurous, it encouraged them to proceed with discretion and hide their entanglements in extra-marital affairs.

Eventually—so I am told—one reaches the age where one can do with or without sex, since the effort devoted to making conquests hardly justifies the ultimate rewards. The final stage—another tale of woe I have had related—will be that one does not even remember what it was like, or how it could be.

Some day I might succumb to the writing of fiction. When I achieve this, steamy sex scenes could well become components of my literary presentations. If this happens, I would leave it to my faithful readers to decide, whether my tantalizingly luscious descriptions of "encounters of a sexual kind" are purely imaginary, or based on personal experiences.

PSYCHICS

As so often, when I express my contentious views about situations that I find peculiar, I promptly succeeded in hurting the feelings of a good friend. She really believes in "experiences of a supernatural kind". While, just like much of religion, I classify psychics in the category of voodoo. You either believe it—when it can indeed help the many adherents—or you do not; and then, as I might some day, you will eventually end up in hell.

Recently I read an article by Timothy Campbell—whoever he is—expressing many of my own apprehensions, with his extremely critical observations in "A Closer Look at Psychics". I promptly passed this along with the query "am I wrong to agree with this guy", and specific questions on what—in my friend's assessment—she had gathered from the Bible, the New Testament, or learned through her religious advisor, about the credibility of psychic revelations and pre-monitions of any kind.

Much more diplomatic in her commentary than I would ever be, she assured me that I was "not wrong" with my *preposterous* assessment—the adjective is mine, not hers—and that she has no problem with my being a sceptic and a non-believer. For herself, though, her "Spiritual Reading" was indeed of great comfort. She also revealed that her Priest was positive about her experience with a fee-for-service guru. She found the consultation consoling, and this—I concur—was of the greatest importance.

We were in complete agreement that, whatever turns you on or off is what you have to live with. And if any of it—no matter how misjudged and critiqued by others—makes you happy, relaxed, reassured, impressed, enlightened, aroused, inspired, entertained, whatever, that much the better.

I would miss the often invigorating debates on differing perspectives that I habitually have with many of my contacts. What could we otherwise review *intelligently*, if we had identical views on everything? It would be so boring.

When I was still in a working environment, I wisely refused to discuss politics, religion, income, a person's age, ancestry, sexual orientation, and a fair number of other subjects—even with friends. I am trying to make up for this long-term lapse in exhilarating interaction. The haste in my current approach can be justified by the—at my age—anticipated limited life-expectancy.

And then it happened to me! It was my first bizarre experience, which somewhat supported my correspondent's viewpoint about psychics.

During an early morning return from *babysitting* (my grandchildren would object to this terminology), I was "innocently" involved and hurt in a serious traffic accident. When I spoke with my kids from home some hours after my release from the hospital, I learned what Kevin, my 12-year old grandson, had related to his Dad that same morning, as he woke up. A dream during the night was about Grandpa being injured in an automobile accident. That was before his father saw my email request to phone as soon as he got up, to eventually find out about my experience.

Only half in jest did I convey this to my friend with "I hope you appreciate the efforts I make to learn about your premonitions". Yet, despite this newly acquired—and continuing as extremely painful—familiarity with the, to me, incomprehensible, I must confess that, on this topic, I am still as mockingly sceptical as ever.

EXERCISING

It is healthy for you. Supposedly makes you live longer, too. I started questioning this axiom long before I learned that some fitness guru, although in excellent condition, had croaked while exercising at a relatively young age. Of course, without his fanatical fitness regime, he might have died even younger. And, to clarify right from the start, I do believe in "living healthy". However, this should not be the most important of your criteria for a happy life. There is such a thing as quality over quantity, which could determine the relative value of the struggle for a longer existence.

Just like everyone else who is not keen on the hardship of enforcing too healthy a lifestyle, I have at least a mental catalogue of people who smoked, drank heavily, and were considerably overweight. They never stood when they could sit; or sat when they could have been lying down. Yet they were still around at a ripe old age.

Mind you, all the smokers among my acquaintances—whatever their other bad habits—have long gone to nicotine heaven. Yet I still encounter obese and mostly immobile people of any age in considerable numbers.

Typical, of course, seems to be that those with weight challenges are the ones who cruise a parking lot to ensure the closest possible space for their car. They are also the ones who consume every bite on a plate that they have within reach. And their favourite restaurants are those with all-you-can-eat buffets. No doubt they find much solace in the t-shirt slogan "Fat people are most difficult to kidnap".

Participation in sports of any kind has never been one of my ambitions. In school I struggled and schemed endlessly to avoid becoming entangled in team efforts or any other personal demonstration of exercising skills. Physical activities "of the sporty type" were always a nightmare. My complete lack of talent and the fear of public ridicule must have been the reason for this abhorrence.

I don't recall what started me on my early morning walks. It might have been some sunny day after my retirement, when Gussie vacuumed the house, and I was trying to escape the racket. It could just as well have been the health-conscious talking heads on television that finally made me decide on regular physical action. During the summer, of course, I had always performed a bit of this when gardening. Yet in winter there was never enough snow to make shovelling a sufficiently recurrent routine.

There is the possibility that this walking craze, which I developed at such a mature age, was a late-blooming hereditary ethnic trait. Germans from the area where I grew up always seemed to be fond of walking. They would take public transportation; or drive at times for considerable distances to park their vehicles; walk vigorously for a couple of hours; and then enjoy a calorie-intensive and cholesterol-raising meal in one of Baden-Württemberg's many splendid rural restaurants. Hold it! I stand corrected, as this could not at all be the reason for my own addiction, since *I am a Canadian*—and never mind the ancestry!

There are folks who take this physical fitness issue seriously. They perform regular weekly or daily work-outs in health spas or fitness institutes. This costs money, of course, which—for such an activity—I refuse to spend. Since I never experienced it, the auxiliary social life of such a structured engagement—hey-hey, might all this be performed in a chick-pick locale?—does not arouse my interest either.

To "break a sweat" and burn up calories, some others erect elaborate equipment in their homes. I have seen such installations, which provide mechanisms for high-tech torture and sophisticated attachments for body-function monitoring; all at great cost. No way, *José!*—(in your mind, to make this rhyme, you should just have intoned the required *Spanish* pronunciation).

Such a solution would also prove expensive. With health-inducing gadgets I never went beyond the acquisition for my spouse of a basic exercyle that I was able to scrounge; and an inexpensive sliding-thingy that, since it regularly gave me backaches, ended up in storage.

The totally cost-free walking schedule became my way out. I have been practicing it religiously for over ten years. If I don't get hit by a falling tree or run over by a passing car in the process, I hope to proceed for another ten years—at least.

Fortunately, in the area where we live, it is quite easy to march on a variety of routes, each of them taking me close to an hour at a vigorous walk. I refuse to jog since—so I read somewhere—this might be overly stressful for my fully matured body.

The daily routine does not depend on the weather. Freezing cold, strong wind, even heavy rain, are no hindrance. Yet I encounter seasonal challenges in the winter, because, for fear of slipping, I refuse to walk outside with even the slightest accumulation of snow or ice on the ground. This can necessitate a number of cancellations between early December and the end of March.

Amazing how, during such a particularly difficult six-week period two years ago, my weight increased considerably without this daily exertion. It progressed to a point where I deemed it crucial to reduce my ingestion of food to compensate for the lack of exercise.

I see many others walking with at least one companion, some in larger groups as well. Even the joggers, while on the road, then pursue a lively conversation. Several are dressed in classy outfits and frequently equipped with the now customary *designer* water bottles—although the content might have come from their home's water faucet. My preference is to go on my own, and I certainly will not succumb to dehydration if I cannot replenish my body's water content until I return home.

Perhaps the preference to walk unaccompanied resulted from my inability to discover anyone living in the area, who would want to accompany me, particularly at my unorthodox early-morning hour. Had there been, such daily togetherness might have evolved into too much of a good thing. My team-mate could have preferred a different speed, route or duration for our joint ventures. I am telling myself—so far convincingly—that I am better off on my own.

Of course, again and again, I do encounter many of the same people. We smile or wave at each other, might even say "Hello" or "Nice Day" or "Cool this morning". Rarely is there a more extensive exchange. The only time that I would ever stop for a chat is if I stumble upon one of my immediate neighbours, whom I had not seen for a while.

It seems that during my walks I operate with a one-track mind—to finish without delay. While normally I am the one who strikes up conversations with total strangers, even just riding in elevators. The possible explanation could be, of course, that, since I usually venture out before breakfast, it is the hunger pangs that encourage me to hasten home.

A "mind your own business" display during walks is not for everyone. Acquaintances of ours, who go for part of my route every day as well, take twice as long as I do to cover half the distance. Of course they stop to chat with many they encounter.

On a couple of occasions, when I happened to catch up with them going in the same direction, I was forced to slow down considerably to let them keep up. During our group activity they were able to relate many tales about this house and that; the people who lived in it now or did before; and what seemed like a short biography of everyone we encountered in transit. They even managed to introduce me to a couple of their regularly encountered fellow-walkers. Not a very useful feat since, when next I passed these formally introduced folks on my own, we merely nodded at each other, as we had always done before.

Not talking to other road-runners does not stop me from observing them. I have encountered several at least a hundred times, whenever we proceed in opposite directions. One chap walks briskly and always looks at me with apparent aggravation; yet a neighbour knows him well and assures me that this is really a very nice chap. A youngish woman crosses over to the opposite side of the street when she sees me coming; once, when I approached her in the company of my then five-year old granddaughter, she escaped from both of us to cross the street. Even our little Emma observed on it at the time. Another chap, a really old geezer—though not quite my age yet—I suspected of being deaf or at least hard of hearing. To test I once asked him at the top of my voice what time it was, to which he responded "yes, very nice", as he had stated on many other days.

Regularly I monitor more "wild-life" than just the human assortment in our neighbourhood. Walkers covering the area later in the day might well miss this exhilaration. At my time of the morning, however, there are always birds; chipmunks and squirrels in large numbers; often Canada geese and seagulls overhead; occasionally foxes, rabbits and racoons; sometimes a skunk; more rarely an opossum or a grouse; on a few occasions I viewed deer as well. And then there are the cats and dogs.

The dogs I encounter are the ones that, ready or not, force their owners—who carry plastic bags—for a walk. If these "doggie bags" are really used to pick up the pets' droppings, I cannot verify. Yet at least they create the right impression with nearby environment-conscious residents.

Media reports about recent attacks by vicious canines have made me a bit apprehensive. When I come across larger specimens on the road, I make eye contact with the owner and not with the animal; keep both hands inside my pockets to preserve all fingers, at least during an initial assault; and clasp my keys in a manner that would assist in my defence, if attacked.

Perhaps I should be more concerned about molestation by humans; particularly on the days when I bank at my branch's *Green-Machine*. The aspects of living dangerously in such situations are covered extensively by the local press. So far I have been fortunate.

Being considered a low-profile target might have something to do with the way I dress. Surely, anyone encountering me in my walking-for-exercise outfits would not deduce that I carry more than a couple of *loonies* for a cappuccino. Let's hope so!

Should I ever get mugged, it will become the subject for another story. If you should be anxiously awaiting my report following such an incident, I must emphasize that I very much hope to be spared, even if I thereby disappoint you!

Garden, Farm and Cottage

My early experience as a gardener was acquired after we moved into our first own home in Roxboro/Quebec. My exposure was very limited, since I had absolutely no interest in such activities.

Once a week at the most—following continuous prodding by my spouse—I cut the lawn, usually while protesting vehemently that "this could surely have waited for another week". Under duress I was also planting some flowers. Poking a broom handle into the ground made holes just large enough to insert the tulip bulbs. Despite continuing lack of Tender-Loving-Care, they bloomed beautifully during the six years of our local residence. Fertilizer, weed killer, insect and grub repellent, mulch, or even water during a lengthy drought, I never applied. Since the soil was clay, interspersed with an ample supply of rocks—explains the community's name *Roxboro*—the grass grew in-between, despite its lack of nurturing.

By the time we moved to Mississauga, I finally developed a taste for the outdoors. Here we had a larger lot, pure sandy soil, and originally nothing but weeds as landscaping. As, indeed, did the neighbours, if they also had just recently moved in.

Our first landscaping investment went for the purchase of evergreen shrubs and trees at a local nursery. At our request, the municipality also planted two linden trees close to the road. Other vegetation we scrounged from friends.

Over many years, we returned with such plants as tamarack trees from Quebec; elephant grass from Nova Scotia; and the beginnings of a wild rose hedge from Germany. As the result of a business trip, I was also able to grow two horse chestnut trees of East European ancestry. After we had acquired our own country property, we transferred more trees and shrubs—even some of our native flowers—from "the farm".

My initial objective was to create, what I called, my "wildlife preserve" on at least part of the property. This area I have been successfully expanding over many years. The main purpose was, of course, to reduce the lawn and flower bed area to a minimum, thereby eliminating the more extensive care they require.

If I had my way, the entire backyard would be—what our grandchildren always called—"the forest". But my spouse will have no part of this! The gradual extensions I had to do secretly, whenever Gussie was out for a while. That's when I sneakily converted another segment into a low-care area. By the time I was found out, it was, of course, too late to stop the manoeuvre.

My outside responsibilities are limited to the development and upkeep of trees, shrubs, perennial flowers, and the lawn. Gussie does the annuals, although I am supposed to keep watering them, whenever they *really* need it.

As a family we are very much into composting. Leaves, garden clippings and some kitchen waste go onto our compost piles; as does a bag of human hair, which—to the puzzlement of her hairdresser—Gussie, on my insistence, requests from him once a year. The entire mixture I keep turning occasionally and—over a two-year period—this decomposes sufficiently to be applied as mulch and nourishment to our flower beds.

My major challenge has always been the lawn; or rather, the *lack of* a decent-looking one. Grubs seem to be the major problem. On two occasions, after failing persistently with my own struggles, I hired commercial lawn-care providers. Over their respective three and two year assignments, they, too, were unable to rid our property of these little critters.

As kids, where I grew up, we knew them as *Maikäfer*. In English, so I learned, they are called *June Bugs*. These allegedly lay eggs, which then develop into grubs and, after ingesting the roots of lawns, they mature into more of the flying insects. On our property, these eggs must all be deposited after my bed-time, because I have never seen even one of the bugs in this area. But I can certainly discover grubs in abundance, whenever I remove any of our decaying grass remnants. As do crows, skunks and raccoons, when digging in our lawn.

Chemicals of any kind, applied to my garden, are very much a "last resort". But, in my struggle—it almost amounts to "psychological warfare"—to rid my grounds of these destructive intruders, I have been spreading granular and liquid poisons over many years, as did the two commercial gardeners, whom I previously employed. All to no avail!

Most home owners in Continental Europe are not known for their English-type lawns. In some countries—Denmark and Germany among them—they generally refrain from watering, fertilizing and—especially—from the application of herbicides or pesticides to their outdoors. Instead of a pure growth of merely grass, they intersperse their greenery with clover and *Gänseblümchen*, locally known as *English Daisies*. From my very biased perspective, this looks really nice. So that could be my next experiment! But do I dare to introduce some new specimen of—what my neighbours could well consider—an invading weed into the local landscape? I'll really have to think about this.

When we progressed to seek our very own place in the country, we wanted nature in a secluded setting, not more than a 90 minutes drive from our home. The more traditional Ontario cottage on a lake, with powerboats racing past and neighbours dropping by regularly, was not our style.

We wanted isolation and only those visitors who had been invited to join us for the day, or indeed for the entire weekend. Once we were established, those who came and, upon arrival, complained too much about the traffic they encountered on the way, or observed nothing but the weeds or the insects once they were there, would not be asked a second time.

It was on August 16th 1971 when we acquired what we would always call "our farm". This fifty-acre property at #7390 Side Road 5 East in Arthur Township was just a few hundred yards (pardon me, this should be *meters*, of course) east of Highway 6 between Arthur and Mount Forest. There were about five acres of cedar bush that adjoined a trout creek; another five acres of hardwood forest, which had previously been a *sugar bush*; and the remaining forty acres of farmland.

Over the next three years, under the terms of the Province's Woodland Improvement Act, the government planted 40,000 (forty *thousand*) trees at one cent per tree for a cost of $400 to us. The species were mainly red pine, white pine and white spruce, but also a few Carolina poplars and red oak, silver maple and, as an experiment in this marginal climate, some 2,000 black walnut trees.

Part of the condition of sale was for the previous owner to transfer to our lot a cabin from an adjoining property that he owned as well. This gave us a comfortable roof over our heads on the many weekends that we spent at the farm.

Gussie quite appropriately referred to our accommodations as "indoor camping". But until Kenneth turned into his teens and would rather spend time with his friends than accompany his parents into the country, we always had a great time.

For quite a number of years we still entertained delusions to build a permanent home, excavate a large pond, even considered to retire there some day. None of this would have been too good an idea, as we realized later. We would have ended up living "in the boonies"; certainly in the *snow-belt area* of Ontario; far away from friends, medical care, even from shopping.

As an absentee landowner you have to expect, I assume, that others trespass. The first encounter that we had was during a weekend stay when, early one morning, I noticed three people at our creek. Once approached, they cheerfully told me that, for as long as they could remember, they had always come from

Hamilton to fish for trout in our waters, as soon as the season started. I had no problem with this, since I neither fish nor eat trout.

Our next experience was with an assortment of beehives that someone had placed onto our property. It took the Ontario Provincial Police to identify this culprit and to have him remove his unregistered and possibly diseased colonies. The state of health of the bees was of serious concern to the "registered" beekeepers in the area. This did not worry me, but, because of my allergy, I was greatly concerned about being stung.

Another trespasser seemed to appear on an annual basis. It was always before the holidays, when this one stole his Christmas trees—plural yet, he must have supplied his friends as well—off our lot. What really annoyed me was that, with thousands to choose from, he often cut them from along our drive, where several of them had been hand-planted by me personally to provide a straight hedge, bordering both sides of the 1,500 foot path to the cabin. In later years, when they had grown beyond the size of a regular Christmas tree, he—perhaps this perpetrator was a she—just cut the tops off some of our specimens.

Over the thirty years of our ownership we had two break-ins at the cabin, with a few minor items pilfered during the first, and some wreckage created during the second incident. Since this also resulted in a broken door and a smashed window, I have since left the place unlocked. A sign at the entrance signals this to potential thieves, vandals or just nosey intruders. On a few more occasions since then, I observed that someone had indeed entered, but without any harm done.

In the deep forest, yet close to the road, we occasionally noted—and still do—the rubbish left by trespassing invaders. The deposits identified the violators as having enjoyed picnics, heavy drinking, even "encounters of a sexual kind".

The most recent intrusion that we discovered was by an assumed hunter. He had the gall to build himself an observation stand in the forest adjoining our creek. I know that this is a really good spot for the observation of deer, since it is also close to the salt-lick that I have been providing for our wildlife over many years. On the stand I left him a note expressing our displeasure, but also the admission that we didn't really know what to do about his encroachment.

In recent years, our own trips to the farm have become rather infrequent. Gussie is not keen on going, and the kids acquired a more luxurious possession to enjoy. This left me for visits on my own. More recently I have been fortunate. Since his retirement, a good friend—a real *lover of the outdoors*, as long as the activities do not extend to "overnighting" away from home—accompanies me two or three times a month for extensive assignments of hard labour.

The newest family weekend retreat is the kids' cottage! "It's Kasshabog, Grandpa, KASSHABOG!" That is what my barely three-year-old granddaughter Emma, with both hands on her hips, emphasized to me on several occasions, when I still had trouble recalling the exact name of their lake.

The locals usually just call it "Lake Kosh"—with an "o", not an "a". Kasshabog must surely be an Indian name, supposedly meaning—who knows what? When it comes to the interpretation of old names, one frequently encounters a variety of explanations. I would not want to vouch for the accuracy of any of them.

The purchase of the cottage might well turn out to be another of our offspring's better investments. On the transfer date of May 25th 2001 they acquired the 1.5 acre property. It has 240 feet of private lake frontage, and a cottage that had been the previous owners' year-round residence.

As part of the original transaction came three boats. There was a canoe, a pedal-boat, and an aluminium boat with an outboard motor. Early that summer, Ken also bought a powerboat from an acquaintance. It was a spotlessly kept and infrequently used 17 foot *Tempest 1980* model equipped with a 165 hp inboard/outboard engine.

Water sports are not among my favourite activities. Once, just the one time for sure, I let my son pilot me around the bay of their lake. For me this was one of those white-knuckle trips, and that despite the life-jacket that I wore. I'll just have to go by the reports of other participants, when they describe in glowing terms how enjoyable it is to careen around the entire body of water at top speed, jumping over the waves created—my two grandsons on wave boards or water skis! Watching them frolic, their little sister, too, while all three are splashing and swimming and diving, makes me lament that I never learned how to be anything other than terrified when on, in, or even just near a body of water.

Back on land, I truly take pleasure in cottage life. I cannot imagine a more relaxing and delightful experience than the view one enjoys while sitting at the dining table, particularly over an elaborate breakfast, my favourite meal of the day. Facing the huge window, one gets a glimpse of the dock and the shoreline, and a grand vista of the bay. The lake in the background is framed by two islands.

There is wildlife in abundance. Beaver and otter swim by; loon and heron catch their fish for a snack; birds and chipmunks are everywhere. Yet the bears—perhaps fortunately—prefer to congregate at the site of the distant garbage dump. Our grandchildren enjoy the chase of the many frogs along the shoreline. There is a hummingbird feeder just outside the kitchen window; almost constantly these tiny birds can be admired as they hover around their dispenser. Game fish, anything suitable for eating, can come from various fishing spots throughout the lake. But it is off the dock, where our grandchildren accomplish their most successful fishing, when an overabundance of rock bass—these do *not* qualify as an edible delicacy—appear from underneath the pier.

There are always some chores that, when I get involved with them myself, I enjoy immensely. Pruning, clipping, cutting and sawing are among my preferred activities. And—just as at the family farm—the cottage will provide me with boundless opportunities throughout my lifetime. On both properties, as well, one can assemble, rearrange, and eventually dismantle and replace many formations of rock and driftwood displays; move floral, shrub, fruit and vegetable plantings; proceed with steps, walks and driveway installations; and also effect repairs and adjustments of the actual buildings. If you look upon any of this as work, you should not have a cottage. For me it is much like "playing around", and I am eagerly anticipating my activities from one visit to the next.

Where there are trees, there are leaves. The more that you have of the first, makes for the *merrier*—perhaps just for the *massive*—volume of the second. Since most of the area's deciduous trees are oak, and these leaves don't seem to decay much during a normal person's lifespan, their removal becomes a significant task. Raking them up is not one of my favourite pursuits. But I do some of it just to be helpful. The one part of this routine that I do get pleasure from, is the burning of the collection, but only as long as I don't think about the smoke pollution that this creates for the environment.

Equally smoky, but the consequence of entertainment rather than work, is the burning of bonfires, something the grandchildren—and the rest of the family—enjoy. We used to do this at the farm when Ken was this young, with the roasting of marshmallows as a definite component of the routine.

There is a new delight, which I heard described but never experienced myself. They call them *Smores*, a concoction of roasted marshmallows, squished between two graham crackers with a piece of chocolate. Sounds very much like my kind of food, and Birte assures me that I will sample some when next I visit at the lake.

Cottaging, with chores of many varieties, can be a full-time job. It fortunately is so for me, since I do not get involved in much of what others consider the "fun part" of their weekends or their summer vacations in the outdoors. I am neither for boating, fishing, swimming, nor for the generous entertainment of masses of friends, relations or mere acquaintances—even of total strangers, whom some of the known visitors bring along.

Some thirty or forty years ago, we derived most of our knowledge of cottage life through the experiences of three separate couples in our age range. Only one of these still continues with the established routine today. It seemed that, for all of them, a large number of visitors regularly materialized with or without invitation. The guests then expected to be taken for boat rides, fed or—the absolute minimum of anticipated hospitality—to be provided with a series of their favourite beverages. If they stayed for the evening's barbeque—and often they did—this typically involved piles of expensive meats and accompaniments. Having provided such entertainment over a number of years, one might well consider the cost of the original acquisition of a property to have been the minor expense.

Our kids assure me that, today's routines—or at least their own arrangements—are much more sensible. They profess to encounter only invited guests; the feeding of the troops is pre-planned, with hosts and overnight visitors taking turns with the provision and the preparation of the meals; and neighbouring cottage people, when they drop by, usually do so with a drink-in-hand from their own supplies.

I never thought this possible. Yet if I am not forced to venture onto the water, I can indeed be a passionate cottager. Of course, I have to be invited before I visit. Gussie, however, as of late, is not that enthusiastic about being anywhere other than in our own home—most of all, she prefers to sleep in her very own bed. My pleasurable experiences, when I can accept our kids' invitations, may therefore not be that frequent.

But on the Thanksgiving weekend, already for the second year in a row, Gussie does indeed come along and enjoys herself as much as anyone. The Thanksgiving festivity at the cottage is really among the annual highlights of our frequent family gatherings. And, as a family, we truly have much to be thankful for, throughout all our years together.

My Career as Hausmann

Even to one who does not speak German, the term *Hausfrau* must seem familiar. And a *Hausmann* is the male equivalent of what the dictionary describes as "mistress of the house" or "housewife".

I recently had to serve in this function over many weeks. It all started when a short visit to the bookbinder, to deliver the material for one of my earlier books, ended in disaster.

Still in the parking lot of this firm's offices in Scarborough, we tried to decide where to go for lunch. That's when Gussie chose to remove her jacket. For some strange reason she felt she had to do this outside the car. As she exited our vehicle, her foot became entangled in the straps of her purse. She stumbled and fell with her full weight onto her right knee.

Her pantyhose, surprisingly, remained undamaged. We should have sold the rights to a commercial, for what was surely a superior product. "Break your knee-cap, but not our pantyhose" might have become the slogan.

Gussie had indeed "fractured the right patella", the medical term that I would hear repeatedly. It looked quite ghastly to me. Where the kneecap used to be, there was an indent; around it three larger chunks of bone; and, at the bottom, an assembly of granules. Predictably, my spouse was in agony.

Should we call for an ambulance? Go to the nearest hospital? Or try to reach the one closest to our residence? We decided on the latter approach. I lifted Gussie into the passenger seat beside me, and made the 45-minute trip to the recently renamed *Mississauga Site* of the *Trillium Health Centre*, just up the road from where we live.

In the Emergency Department we were admitted quickly, saw a doctor-on-duty, eventually the specialist and, following examinations, X-rays, and the completion of the paperwork, had the operation scheduled for the late evening.

Gussie was brave throughout the entire ordeal. Following what, in the words of the surgeon, was a "successful operation", she was released from the hospital and into my care after a three-day stay. That's when I began my new career as *Hausmann*.

We live in a three-level home. The kitchen, the living room, and the dining area are on the main floor. Up seven steps are three bedrooms and both bathrooms, which also incorporate the toilets. And since my spouse could not navigate any stairs, that presented a considerable challenge.

With a rearrangement of most of the furniture in the area, and the rental of the necessary equipment, we furnished the former dining room with a hospital bed and a commode (that's a fancy name for a portable toilet). We also rented a wheelchair (that we never used) and a walker.

The installation of an extra cable outlet allowed for television viewing from Gussie's temporary location. A cordless telephone, quickly arranged by our son, let her communicate easily from the hospital bed.

To help her in and out of bed during the night, I needed a wake-up call. A dinner bell, our first means of communication, did not create enough noise for this purpose. There were also a few "false alarms", when I had mistakenly responded to the tinkling of our outdoor wind chimes. This necessitated the provision of a real noisemaker, the lid off one of our frying pans, and a wooden cooking spoon to serve as the drumstick.

We both had much moral support from friends and relations. Cards, letters, emails and telephone messages arrived daily. The many offers of actual help, we tried to discourage as much as possible.

Most of Gussie's cheering section came from the immediate family, with our wonderful grandchildren Steven, Kevin and the baby Emma. At just over four years of age at the time, Kevin was the most upset of all. He just couldn't fathom that his beloved Omi, who until then had always been very active in playing with him, was all of a sudden bed-ridden and in visible discomfort. It took him quite a while to accept the new situation.

The assignment of "chief cook and bottle washer" became mine. To do the regular—and many irregular—daily tasks, I needed simplified routines. This began on day one, when I disappointed some of our local friends who brought flowers. They either had not received or did not believe my announcement to everyone that additional plants would be a nuisance, and not at all welcome. I refused acceptance of such well-intentioned presents. Surely there were enough chores already.

My telephone instructions were too late for two floral arrangements, which arrived from Europe. I was forced to retain them but, with the limited care that they received from me, I was fortunate in being able to discard the little beauties after only a couple of days.

Our existing houseplants were assembled on the kitchen table. Close enough to each other that I could service them quickly.

Dishes and cutlery, all that we would ever have to use during this period, were washed right after meals and left in the sink to dry; until they were needed again, when this ritual was repeated.

At long last, I was able to organize some of the kitchen cupboards according to my preferences. Whatever I used throughout my special assignment ended up on the lower shelves of the upper cabinets, not higher than eye level. I neither stretched nor bent to get anything from then on.

Not that there was much cooking to do, anyway. Breakfast and a light lunch were the very simple routines that we had always followed. Dinner I was able to get from a variety of fast-food places. It took me a while to persuade friends that the provision of prepared meals was indeed well intentioned, but for me merely an additional chore to heat and serve. It also resulted in more dishes for washing. And this was something that I preferred not to have to endure.

For laundry, I received precise instructions from my patient on how to proceed. But ironing was something that would have to await Gussie's full recovery. I had never understood why bed sheets, towels, pyjamas or underwear needed pressing. Yet to avoid stocking the closets with wrinkly items, I used the same outfits again and again. There was no one objecting—or even noticing—that we had the identical, albeit frequently washed, linen, towels and underwear throughout the entire period.

The shopping routine was much simplified as well. I did not go to a variety of stores to buy what was perhaps the best or the freshest or the cheapest. All my purchases came from one supermarket.

When the surgeon removed the 23 staples applied during the operation, a synthetic cast, reaching the full length of the leg, was applied. After this cast was removed some weeks later, the rehabilitation, which eventually also included pool therapy—we called it "water ballet"—commenced for two performances each week. Gradually thereafter, Gussie became mobile again and, with much determination and initially also considerable pain, was able to manage our stairs as well. Eventually she had progressed sufficiently that whatever therapy was needed, she could do at home on her own. The ultimate measure of progress was when, finally, she again drove her own car.

It was a full year since the accident, when the final operation for this predicament, the "removal of patella hardware", could be completed. Then, with a mere few more days of recuperation under my expert *Hausmann* care, my beloved wife was again "as good as new", or even better!

HOW ARE YOU

Most people addressed with "How are you" will reply "Fine and how are you"—no matter what ails them at the time. They recognize this query as a greeting. The question is not meant to elicit an announcement about anyone's physical or emotional state. At times, I respond with an atypical "Why do you have to ask, don't I look good", which surely most take as a joke.

Rarely does one encounter someone who considers the initial inquiry as something serious, feeling compelled to respond with a lengthy report about his or her wellbeing—or lack thereof. Then a lesson will have been learned that such an innocent should never again be approached with "How are you".

Instead one might say "Great day, isn't it", and that even if it is raining or snowing or windy and minus 20 degrees. Those who know the game would—in incremental weather—recognize the intended humour in the statement, and reply accordingly. But there are still some folks who could take all this literally. They would provide detailed commentary about the weather they experienced, not only on the day in question, but also during previous seasons when conditions might have been better or worse.

An occasional expression today, at least among teenagers, seems to be "Whazzup", to which the appropriate reply follows as "Whazzup" as well. I like this for a colloquial exchange because, with merely two words, the case is closed, and one can advance to something really meaningful.

Regularly I attend my annual high school reunions. We have an inferred understanding that diagnosis of your own health, or bragging about your grandchildren, are taboos for general discussion. Acceptable would be the brief report to the group on someone else's handicap, to explain their absence at the time. As an attendee, it would also be appropriate to reveal your own situation to your closest friends, but only in a one-on-one chat. I must admit that, not introducing the latest pictures of my grandchildren to those present has proven a challenge. I am tempted—but have not yet succumbed—to show off my little darlings, from a collection of photos that I carry with my pocket calendar.

With former colleagues from my last employer, we assemble twice each year. Fortunately, there are very few of the regular participants, who have the strange notion that—without even being asked the magic question—they should reveal in gruesome detail everything that ever happened to them in an infinite number of "encounters of the medical kind". During the pre-lunch reception, you try to move away from them quickly. And you pity the poor soul who sits next to them for the duration of the meal.

Is it a Chinese maxim that conveys "Ask the question, you seem uninformed once; do not ask the question, you remain ignorant always"? But surely they never intended this to solicit a medical bulletin from a simple "How are you" greeting.

GAMBLING WITH INVESTMENTS

If you want to become *very-very* rich, you might consider exactly the opposite of my more daring experiments over the years. To be really safe, it would also help if you started by being wealthy, just in case this reverse scheme brings no success, either.

I must emphasize, right from the start, that I think investments in the stock market, just like any other kind of gambling, should never be with funds that you cannot afford to lose. If you consider failure as a possibility, and are capable of absorbing eventual losses, then you can get enjoyment out of your often foolish decisions.

On three occasions I accepted the "expert" advice from friends, who professed to know what they were doing. They—as they had bragged for years—were extremely successful with their own stock ventures. I should have learned from the very first one of these eventual ordeals.

Reacting to "hot tips", no matter what their alleged temperature, is a suckers' game. In each instance, the sizeable—by my standards—initial investments fizzled away into mere penny stocks. Of course, on the predicted upside, I could have benefited greatly, had the much touted schemes worked out.

These were my biggest individual losses over the years—along with NORTEL, of course, that became noteworthy all by itself. I am glad (am I really?) that the company's executives and directors did well if they sold any of their holdings close to the high point; but, without "insiders' information", it didn't work this way for me. Yet, who am I to begrudge them the many millions they took off their sinking ship.

My career as a gambler—I could also say "investor"—started when we still lived in Montreal some forty years ago. At that time, I bought the odd *Irish Sweepstakes* ticket. On one occasion I even won just over three hundred dollars. Since gambling was illegal in Quebec—although widely practiced then as it is now—the transfer of the winnings from Ireland came to me via a private address in Bermuda, some months after the draw.

In Ontario, ever since the start of the Provincial Lottery, we have been supporting our government with $3 each week to acquire tickets for both *Lotto* and *Lottario*. Rarely did we have a winner, and then only either $5 or $10.

At times—usually in combination with the purchase of gasoline at a service station—I also splurge $5 for a Win-a-Million ticket. On several occasions this resulted in small prices, which I immediately reinvested into more of the same tickets—ensuring revenue for the Province, but, alas, naught for me. However, since these are of the scratch-to-win variety, I occasionally wondered if, with a high-tech screening device, some clever culprit could not scan them for possible big wins before they ever went on sale.

Just for the fun of it, I have visited—each of them but once—casinos in Britain, Germany, Monaco, Sweden, the USA and Yugoslavia; as well as our very own government-revenue-creator in Niagara Falls, Ontario. My preferred game was *roulette*. The maximum amount that I ventured has always been the local currency equivalent of $50 Canadian.

I do have a "very sophisticated" system. Some system! I never left with any winnings, and it seldom took me very long to exhaust all my allocated funds. Whether I really had $50-worth of entertainment is debatable.

Ventures in the stock market proved equally unspectacular with their rewards. I still continue to explore different approaches, yet none of them led to the big one—as yet.

Mutual Funds were my earliest endeavour. Once I recognized the percentages of the management fees assessed, and the not more than average returns, I dispensed with most of these. There are only two or three in a present portfolio, which I have retained "for sentimental reasons".

Next came the exploration of big-cap blue chips, primarily those with a DRIP (Dividend Reinvestment Plan) and an OPP (Optional Purchase Plan). Following the *mantra* of investment guru Warren Buffett, I obtained them for the long-term. I still retain and keep augmenting most, which rewards me with both dividends and capital growth in a satisfactory manner.

"Investing for Couch Potatoes" sounded interesting, when I reviewed its historical performance. My choice of appropriate Index Funds did well over the years I had them.

Most of my selections appear on the Home Page of my computer screen, whenever I turn it on. This can annoy or thrill me throughout the day, as I monitor the progress, deterioration, or—hopefully never—the total demise of any of my investments. Yet my only meaningful accounting comes but once each year, after the end of March. That is when I assess, compare, analyze, augment, reduce, transfer, or sell components of various stocks.

Amounts invested through a full-service broker worked alright over many years; although the learned advice of the expert usually returned no more than the average of my other portfolios. But, then again, there is always hope for the current year, and we haven't reached the day of judgement yet. The fate of my guru, as that for the other mutations of my portfolios, has to be determined next April 1st, as it is every year.

I have the most fun with what I call my *play money*, traded over the Internet through a discount broker. True, there were—to me "considerable"—losses at the very beginning, when I reacted to the hot-lead suggestions previously mentioned. But all of these I regained long ago as the result of more profitable transactions.

To simplify the eventual settlement of my estate, I may well decide to convert all my stocks into fixed-rate and guaranteed investment packages during my eightieth year—assuming that I last that long. Should I depart before, someone else will have to sort it out for the final tax declaration. Hopefully, either my target date or my earlier demise will not be during a year with a bear market. You can wish me luck!

EGO CORPORATIONS

The heading for this article is my translation of *Ich A.G.,* where the *A.G.* component is the abbreviation for *Aktiengesellschaft,* a Limited Company. In Germany, an *Ich A.G.* often describes those among growing numbers of individuals, who either lost or gave up previous employment. Rather than becoming an "unemployed" statistic, they then register their very own one-owner-no-staff firms.

In Canada, too, I am occasionally presented with business cards identifying a bearer as President, Chairman, General Manager, or with some other illustrious title, for an organization in this *I-Ltd.; Me-Inc.;* or *Ego-Corp.* category.

Where these establishments serve the purpose of a tax advantage, it makes a great deal of sense. Unfortunately I am not in a position where, with such an arrangement, I could reduce my payments to the not always prudent recipients of my tax dollars at federal, provincial, regional and municipal levels. I would just love to deduct from my taxable income a part of the cost of my accommodation, automobile leasing, travel expenses, even imaginary salary payments to members of my family. No such luck!

Others launch themselves with the intent and—I sincerely wish them success with their endeavours—the occasional dire need to supplement meagre pensions to just "make ends meet", while freelancing or in contract assignments. This is also a commendable effort, which I am fortunate enough not to have to pursue.

A third group, of mere *eager beavers,* comprises people who never "worked to live", but actually saw their calling as a "live to work" compulsion. They would indeed quickly deteriorate both mentally and physically, if they could not continue with their real or imaginary careers until their final exodus to the great hereafter. This, too, I can understand and, as long as it makes them happy, who am I to critique?

Amusing to me are the show masters. They still own a suit and tie, which may make them feel like entrepreneurs; qualify for none or very little in tax deductions, since they generate no worth-while financial rewards; and have no need of additional income for their well-being. But—and this seems to be the reason for their involvement—they like to pass themselves off as busy individuals, in a variety of ventures that they can brag about. These I consider as poor souls, who obviously have no *real life.*

Since my retirement, I am in the fortunate position to occasionally wonder—like some others, although usually in jest—how I ever found time to go to work, while still employed. I also can't think of even one person whom I would want to impress with a fancy title on a business card.

Occasionally I hear our kids muse about the advantages of my taking on a new job, at least as a part-time assignment. They try to be kind to Gussie, of course. They figure that, getting me out of the house more often, could be a real treat for my beleaguered spouse.

I will need more convincing arguments than merely the emotional well-being of my beloved. Yet, if and when I ever get into the situation where I want to become occupied beyond all my current assignments, I could well see myself as a dollar-a-year supporter of some worthy cause—but not a charity. At that time, however, I might be disappointed by the complete lack of interest from possible employers. This would make it their loss, of course, much more than mine.

OUR LEGAL SYSTEM

Last November, during their absence on vacation, my cousin's home was burglarized. The perpetrators took electronic equipment and other items, along with the family's valuables and documents, the content of a 300-pound safe. They removed this from the basement, and then transported their entire loot in the family's also stolen car.

Two days after discovery of the crime, the automobile was involved in a hit-and-run accident on Highway 401. The driver of the other vehicle, the one they hit, and from which at least one of the occupants required hospitalization, noted three men and a woman in the offending car. He assured police that he could definitely identify the driver.

Once the customary waiting period had expired, the insurance company paid for a "total loss" on the missing automobile. Shortly thereafter, the authorities located it. Once they had examined their discovery—looking for fingerprints or other traces of the culprits, perhaps—they called to invite the former owners to collect any personal items still in the car.

All that remained was a container in the trunk, which my cousin and her husband had used for the transportation of groceries. Inside was a letter from the Parole Board, addressed to an individual living in their general area. It very courteously reminded this Young Offender about several missed appointments with his Probation Officer. It also advised him of a possibly required future court appearance on "Wilful Failure to Comply" charges. This message must have *really* concerned this outstanding young man, who—my fault and that of our society, much more than his own, I suspect—had no doubt chosen a life of crime because of an unhappy childhood!

Full of expectations for the immediate arrest of the culprit and the recovery of some of their heirlooms and especially their documents, my relatives presented the letter to the police. They were disappointed to learn that, by itself, this could not bring about a suspect's apprehension. Since surely, any thief, who ever watched a crime show on TV, would be able to claim that he never saw it before, and that some evildoer had merely planted it to frame him.

Thanks to the good memory of the violated driver from the 401 incident, the opportunity for an arrest finally presented itself. From a number of photographs shown to him, this good citizen pointed out the offending criminal. Progress at last—so we thought!

Through perusal of this case I decided to observe the practice of our legal system. It became a very frustrating experience. What I saw of my tax dollars at work did not impress me.

I was not an observer at what might have been the arrest and then an earlier hearing, during which the suspected burglar, thief, hit-and-run driver, parole-violator, was released without bail "on his own recognizance". The reportedly qualifying factor seemed to be that he had a permanent residence—or at least an address for some such place. This might have automatically made him a solid citizen!

On January 16th I attended a Court Hearing. Once they called the alleged culprit's name, he moved up front from the audience—where I, too, had been sitting—and there some unidentified woman stood up and declared that he had decided to get himself a lawyer. The justice and some other players—including the accused, politely addressed as "Sir"—agreed on a future date. The entire routine had taken less than a minute.

On February 13th, my cousin and her husband sat in during the proceedings themselves. This time, when "Sir" stood before the bench, he was asked about a lawyer. He mentioned that, only the week before, he had spoken to such a distinguished representative, but—for reasons unknown—his defender had not appeared in court. As a result, the presiding justice of the peace, following consultation with the accused, scheduled another date.

I surmised that such a lawyer would be provided from my taxes under the legal aid system; that the accused was without a job and lived on welfare, again from my tax support; that he had to keep on stealing cars to provide a means of transportation; and that—to further augment his income—he was forced to continue with burglaries. Do I sound too cynical?

On March 6th I was present at another one of these performances. Once his name was called, the assumed criminal and three of those staffing the front lines mumbled to each other. These performers in the continuing tragicomedy might have been lawyers, prosecutors, recording clerks, or mere schedule keepers. The outcome of their deliberations was the announcement that a defence lawyer under the legal-aid program was not yet available. Another gathering, following approval of the proposed date by the accused, was then scheduled.

During the early part of the proceedings, several others, already incarcerated in a penal institution, appeared "by video"—as they called it. Their questioning was similar to that later done for the general *clientele* sitting in the courtroom. Since the routine eliminated the need for their personal transfer to the proceedings—with a police escort, yet—I considered this the first manifestation of efficiency. Yet the need for their questioning on the screen, at such a pedestrian level, seemed to me as dubious as that of most of the other culprits who appeared in person.

Two "prisoners"—one at a time—presented themselves in person. They were in handcuffs and accompanied by a police officer, who looked young enough to still be in high school. Their hearing was as brief and seemed as unnecessary as that of just about everyone else this entire morning.

March 17th was the next event in this never-ending saga. Certainly not to my surprise, the perpetrator indicated that he was awaiting the outcome of his legal aid application, and another hearing was scheduled for two weeks hence.

They must have processed some 75 reviews, before "my guy" was called. The time it took for most cases was about thirty seconds (thirty *seconds!*). Most of the accused were just being remanded for a later date.

Interpreters for these thirty-second hearings accompanied several of the suspects. I assume that such linguists receive—again from my taxes—at least a minimum amount for each attendance.

I began to wonder if legal aid lawyers collect their compensation based on the number of appearances forced upon their clients. It was amusing to observe the reaction of one such lawyer who—after being handed a two-page document under "disclosure"—requested a four-week delay for the next hearing, to allow him to study the information. He must have been a slow reader!

Over a period of weeks, my prime suspect had a few more scheduled thirty-second hearings, with customary adjournments to a later date until—who can blame him—"my man" became a no-show. That is when a bench warrant was issued for his arrest.

Several months have passed since then, and the bench warrant is still outstanding. No one seems to be looking for him or, if done at all, this has not been a success. It was his alleged "permanent residence" that initially allowed his release without bail; I wonder if anyone went looking for him there.

When captured on any new charges, the outstanding warrant *should* automatically become known. Such information on the National Police Data Bank supposedly identifies his earlier misdeeds, even if—as an example—his next arrest occurs in British Columbia. Our authorities in Ontario, however, might then not be prepared to cover the expense for his escorted transportation to the Province of his previous crimes. This would free him right after his predicament for the more recent misdeeds had been resolved.

With my somewhat tainted view of this world, I suspect that he might well operate with several aliases, undisturbed despite a previous record or perhaps several outstanding warrants under his various names. It would allow him to continue his life of crime despite the law enforcement authorities' sophisticated computer databases.

Does this sound reasonable?

STRUGGLING WITH POLITICS

After I had retired, while Mike Harris was running for Premier of Ontario, I became a financial contributor to his party's candidate in my electoral district. Both the Premier and my local representative were successful. It was one of the rare occasions when, with my—albeit never before *financial*—political support, I had chosen a winner. From January 8th 1995, the Harris government replaced the aberration of Ontario's first-ever Socialist regime under Bob Rae, which the Province had endured during the preceding four years.

With Harris I experienced a party leader who, once in power, successfully implemented almost everything he had promised during his campaigns. Customarily, the offerings of "bribes to the constituents with their own money" are presented by all candidates before the votes are cast, to be quickly forgotten once the rascals are elected. To see delivered what a politician had promised was an amazing feat. I was really impressed! Unfortunately, Mike Harris could not remain in charge forever.

During both his provincial elections, I had displayed "Vote Conservative" signs on my front lawn. With their current leadership, and a—from my perspective—much weakened conservative thrust, I will not do this again when next we go to the polls.

My earlier monetary support for the local MPP had brought me an actual membership in the Provincial Conservative Party. When Harris retired, this came to haunt me. During the leadership campaign I was inundated with letters; emails; 'phone calls; even personal visits by campaign workers; for all the aspirants.

The eventually anointed successor as party leader—which also made him Premier of the Province—despite his Conservative label, might as well have been a Liberal, judging by his actions. Of course, as normally happens to me, for the party's leadership, too, I had supported an eventual "second choice" candidate.

While I am not happy with the Tory's new #1, I fully recognize that he was probably the more likely—or the less unlikely—to have his party continue in power after the next provincial election, if at all. My own "hero"—because of his more right-of-centre views, much closer to my own—wouldn't have had any chance with the currently prevailing mood of an always fickle electorate.

Throughout my working life, I was not allowed to demonstrate any partisan views in public. It was almost a condition of employment that, politically, I had to prostitute my revealed opinion on a continuing basis. I particularly found this necessary under the four-year tenure of the *NDP's* socialist flock. It was understood that, in order to retain employment, I was to loyally serve my masters; and this I did, whatever their political ilk. The alternative would have been to resign, and I never felt *that* strongly about the situation.

For the most recent federal election, I had made the Canadian Alliance my choice. While I deplored the transfer of their leadership from Preston Manning—he was "my kind of guy"—to Stockwell Day, I voted for their party nevertheless. Had I carried this partisan support to the display of election signs on my lawn—something that my wife had persuaded me *not* to do—I might have been really embarrassed after the election, when the party's newest leader turned out to be such a dud.

As it applies to political choices, I can be rather imbecilic, when I bestow my favours onto someone, because he or she most vigorously opposes the one I am against. With me as a supporter at voting time, more often than not, it guarantees the defeat of "my" candidate or—in the unlikely event that I chose a winner—it produces one of the least impressive administrations in recent history. At least federally, this has been the case.

When we still lived in Quebec, there was no choice but the Liberals, if one was among the Anglos or an *Allophone*. After our move to Ontario, Pearson was my man, because he opposed Diefenbaker, whose mannerisms made me wince. I was enthusiastic about Trudeau, although he created many of today's problems, so I fully realized much later. Chrétien became my initial choice *only* because he was *not* with the party of Mulroney, whose schmaltzy blarney had turned me off. Grudgingly I must admit today, that many of the "Irish baritone's" implementations were not that bad. Then I tried to put my "trust"—who am I kidding—into the Canadian Alliance, in the hope of reducing the Liberals to a minority government. And all to no avail.

Gussie is politically much more astute than I have ever been. Yet, her sound advice does not persuade me very often. It is usually after the fact, when I recognize that she was right—or at least less wrong than I. However, the candidate, for whom she eventually votes, she always keeps a secret—even from me!

Then, with another election on the horizon, I did it again! I let myself get suckered into a political affiliation, and all this despite the family history. This time it resulted in an association with a federal party. My financial contribution, in support of one of their aspirants to become the party's candidate in our electoral district, involved me beyond my initial intentions.

Media commentary on the one I assessed as being worthy of my support made me mail him a cheque. Either one of his two opponents could—in my somewhat unapprised judgment—become at best an "also ran" against the ruling party's incumbent.

One of those competing with "my man" for my chosen party's nomination was a one-time cabinet minister with, what appeared to be, extensive ethnic ties and such support in the community. Of course, anything to do with our multiculti *apartheid* shenanigans is what I greatly abhor.

My favourite had an interesting business background; long-time family ties in our area; active involvement in community affairs; and did not—now we get to the important part—harp on any loving relationship with ethnic, racial, cultural or religious groups. So far so good!

Financial support to the campaign had brought me the customary party membership. This entitled me to attend the riding's Nomination Meeting. I went because it coincided with my "you *gotta* do everything once in your life" penchant; it would let me further assess my preferred candidate; and, once reassured, I could indeed cast my ballot for him.

Media reports later revealed that there were 1,700 registered memberships for the riding's association. In the large hall where the meeting was held, there must have been close to a thousand attendants.

To enter I had to identify myself with a personal document, my driver's license. I observed that this was not demanded from all. I might have been the token representative of what used to be our *Leitkultur,* to show those from other groups that there was no discrimination, since even I, as the obviously harmless "old white guy in a suit", was examined. To let me pass, they also viewed my party membership card, and sought my assurance that I had indeed personally paid the $10 fee.

The registration appeared as a badly organized routine. Without a serious commitment to the process—mine to do this but once; others perhaps from conviction that it was a worthy cause—one might well have turned around and missed the main event.

At three locations within the hall, clearly identifying the sponsors, the competing candidates provided free coffee for their faithful. I passed on this since, considering the milling crowd, spilling it while being jostled was a real possibility.

Following an unexciting introduction by the chairman, each candidate made his spiel. My chap was indeed the superior performer; the "ethnic guy" at his—certainly from my viewpoint—despicable best; while the third aspirant I just vaguely recall as not a memorable presenter.

Then came the actual casting of the ballots. I had the good fortune to be within a few feet of the adjoining room, where the booths were set up. When the presentations concluded, and attendees rushed to vote and quickly get home for their preferred TV-saga, the scrutineers were not yet prepared. This resulted in a large crowd thronging in the hallway outside the locked doors and backing up into the community hall.

After what appeared like a ten-minute wait, they finally started admitting the restless attendees. As the fifth in line to enter, I cast my ballot and went home. The general inconvenience of it all discouraged me from milling about until—perhaps hours later—there might have been a second ballot, if one of the candidates did not receive an absolute majority on the first.

The following day I learned that my preferred contender had indeed won on the first ballot, and with a substantial majority. It was also revealed that a mere 471 votes were submitted. I could only assume that—considering the delay and the somewhat daunting mob scene—many of those who attended the preceding meeting might have departed without actually voting.

The press later revealed some of the tribal tomfoolery arranged by the *multiculti* guy, that I found appalling. Among other things he had invited his supporters to a party, at which a colour TV; a video recorder; a CD/DVD player; and a portable stereo; were given as door prizes. I would not be surprised if the religious leaders of his ethnic group, in their Sunday sermons, had also been encouraging their faithful to support "one of their own".

What I learned since then is that, to partake in the selection process for a party's candidate, you do not have to be either a citizen or of an age, which could qualify you as a registered voter in the ultimate election. Verification of residence within the electoral district is vague at best. Real or professed "legal immigrants" qualify, as long as they are 14 years of age. This would explain the youngsters in the crowd, and the large number of clannish women who—in a patriarchal culture—might have been firmly directed on how to vote by the family elder. Surely this was done in their native language, because I detected that many did not converse in English.

Since then, I have written to the party and to Election Canada offices, to recommend, that only those entitled by law to vote in an election should be permitted to participate in a nomination meeting. Yet, since the government in power seems to be benefiting most from the busloads of ethnic voters, I doubt if they take an interest in such a change. This is another malfunction of our political system with which I have to live.

Of course, again at this election, my support proved the equivalent of "the kiss of death". My party's candidate did not win when the federal votes were cast shortly afterwards. As the eternal optimist, however, I still have hope for him the next time around, as early as within a year or two, since we currently have a minority government. I even retained his election sign to post on my front lawn. I assume, of course, that by then his party will still be deserving of my support.

THE GOVERNOR GENERAL

She may well turn out to be one of the more memorable Governors General that we ever had. And again, she may not. I somehow hope that, as the twenty-seventh Canadian representative of our Head of State, her eventual eminence or notoriety will not result from having been the very last one. But everything is possible.

Soon this lady will be known as *Her Excellency the Right Honourable* Michaëlle Jean. Not bad for a mere broadcaster from Radio-Canada's French-language program in Quebec, until her designation totally unknown in nine of our ten Provinces and in our three Territories.

This latest appointee being a woman (we had a few of these before); or an immigrant from Haiti (many of her predecessors were immigrants as well, or assignees dispatched to "govern" us by the mother country, the United Kingdom); or as an *Afro-Canadian* being a member of a visible minority (the current incumbent, whom she replaces, is an ethnic Chinese); are of no concern. However—as usual I am being overly critical—her being a mere "personage of insignificance" disturbs me greatly; as does the French citizenship that both she and her husband still retain—for which she allegedly applied *after* she had become a Canadian.

Appointments to this post are made by her Majesty Queen Elizabeth II, whom the Governor General then represents in Canada. It is always *on the recommendation of* the Prime Minister in power. Objections by the Royals in London might well be voiced before the candidate selected becomes known to the public. Yet I am not aware of previous rejections. Theoretically, therefore, our governing "masters" in Ottawa, once we elect them to power, can nominate and secure confirmation for any political *wanna-be* or *has-been* of their choice. They might have done this on occasion.

However, most of those previously in this illustrious position had at least *some* semblance of a notable career; often a verification of their service to Canada; and always, it seemed, a commitment to our nation. None of the media reports to date have revealed any such virtues for this lady.

The possibility of separatist leanings is also a concern. Perhaps she, and most certainly her French-born spouse—a film-maker who reportedly considers himself an "intellectual"—have associated with those seeking a separation of Quebec from the rest of Canada. In his case, the media's well-documented fraternization was with previously convicted terrorists of the infamous FLQ.

Of course, one does foolish things in one's early life, which—among full reflection when one has reached a later level of maturity—one finds incomprehensible. Some of my own youthful aberrations come to mind.

Within a Franco environment in Quebec, I can well see myself contemplating the benefits of independence for "my nation", since I see separation as the only guarantee for the retention of French culture and language. Possible economic disadvantages could be a bearable by-product of living in *my own country.*

It seems that I just made the case, that possible earlier separatist leanings of *Her Excellency* and *His Excellency*—shortly her spouse will be so addressed as well—can be forgiven.

That leaves me with but two points of grave concern. To have an apparent "lightweight" selected for the vice-regal position, from among more than thirty million Canadians; and the question of additional citizenship of a foreign country. The French nationality is particularly disconcerting, since it is of a country from where certain elements—most distressingly their former President Charles deGaulle—have always been stirring the cauldron of separatist unrest in *our Canadian Province* Quebec.

Media coverage on the day of the initial announcement prominently displayed a photograph of the Prime Minister, along with the GG-designate, her husband and their daughter. I felt compelled to email the PM's office on August 5th 2005 with this message:

Mr. Prime Minister, there must be a government program, which will reimburse the spouse of the newly anointed Governor General for the purchase of a baseball cap. It would enhance the classy appearance of the natty t-shirt that he wears on the front-page picture of this morning's National Post. Her Majesty, whom his wife will represent, will surely be impressed whenever they meet.

Needless to say there has been no acknowledgement.

Cynic that I am—albeit a usually very happy one, so I must stress—my assessment of our universe suspects some sinister motive in the current selection process. Perhaps the appointment of "persons of mediocrity" demonstrates that, in today's Canada, the position of Governor General has become one of irrelevance. Just as our ties with the Monarchy in general are something that many Canadians might prefer to relinquish.

My exposure to the institution has merely been from a tourist's perspective. My wife and I visited Rideau Hall on a number of occasions; usually when we guided some out-of-country visitors. They were then astonished that we "still live under an *English* Queen". Earlier this month, while visiting Ottawa with my grandson Kevin, the tour of the GG's residence was part of our itinerary as well.

Years before a predecessor's appointment was made, I had occasional professional contact with a later Governor General—the one who now, for a few more weeks, remains as our soon retiring emissary of Her Majesty. Those who knew her from our previous working environment, found her selection at the time perfectly in order. She was, after all, a person of accomplishment and perfect poise. Some snickered, however, suggesting that, becoming a "mere representative" of the Queen was no career advancement, since she had always considered herself royalty in her own right.

When Gussie and I became Canadian citizens, the oath of allegiance was to her Majesty Queen Elizabeth and *her heirs and successors*. At the time I was not sufficiently familiar with the other royals, and could not foresee the further development of our Queen's progeny. That explains why I enthusiastically uttered my oath with full conviction.

Since then I discovered a few of our current crop, who fit the pattern of some royals in monarchies world-wide, either as rascals or morons—sometimes both. In principle I am also against hereditary titles or inherited roles of any kind.

Yet what are possible alternatives to a vice-regal head of state, is what I have asked myself on occasion. I would have no momentous objections if, with the demise of the current Queen, we would disband the Governor General position, and part with the continuation of the British—to me it's the English, really—monarch's identification as *our Canadian* King or Queen. At the same time, however, I would greatly deplore the elimination of yet another one of the very few remaining historical cultural ties to our glorious past, that I have come to cherish; thereby making way for ever more of the "politically correct" *multiculti* tomfoolery that I abhor.

For Head of State we then might surely be guaranteed a continuous array of voter-induced rejects from active politics, appointed by the Head of Government as a reward for service to *the party* rather than *the country*. Just as I suspect that—despite the denials of any political affiliation by the latest entrant—Mme. Jean's selection, at least in the views of our Prime Minister's Office, was entirely for political reasons. Although I doubt if it will really assist the current Martin team during the next election, with voters of French or Black extraction.

There is a variety of selection processes in vogue within other countries. Yet, I have detected none so far, that would improve what we have experienced ever since Confederation. Perhaps, still during my lifetime, someone will make a serious effort to evaluate alternatives. When this is done and the system changes, it will not make everyone happy, either.

My preference for our Head of State—with or without a royal connection—would always be for someone who is Canadian by birth; has no other citizenship; communicates articulately in both our official languages; was outstanding in an impressive career; and leaves absolutely no doubt about his or her loyalty to our nation. Their gender; sexual orientation; race; original ethnicity; religion; or geographic home-base in Canada; should not be a consideration. I would also expect, that they and their spouses, whatever their ancestry, would be suitably attired when they present themselves in public. Then at least I could be content.

Hero Worship

Our heroes today seem of a different breed. Perhaps my genuine understanding of the issue is hindered by a merely superficial vetting of the subject's media coverage. While I detect such commentary on a daily basis, I limit myself to the headline, an examination of any highlighted segment, and—only on rare occasions—an admittedly skimpy perusal of the detailed material.

Yet watching television news and, occasionally observed, the professed sagacious commentary of the talking heads, I feel that I have enough awareness of a topic to voice an opinion. At times, too, just a scanty inspection helps me decide that I am better served *without* a personal stance.

A recent CBC promotion asked viewers to identify their all-time Canadian hero. The eventual champion was a socialist politician from the Prairies, whom we credit as the instigator behind our national health plan. I am, of course, very happy to have this medical benefit, which is available to everyone. But I also feel that making him the *numero uno* of Canadian heroes is a bit of overkill—with no medical pun intended.

The second choice of the Canadian Broadcasting Corporation's viewers, I found rather amusing. Perhaps it made the point about how preposterous the entire survey really was. It brought Don Cherry to the foreground. His reputation is that of a loud-mouthed, controversial, red-neck hockey commentator.

Since I do not watch the sport, I merely encounter him on his sporadic TV and radio commercials and during the occasional media interview after he made another shocking pronouncement that needed amplification. In his case it would never be for an apology or a withdrawal of his frequently offensive pronouncements—often right to the point, *my* point that is. Had I cast a ballot during this process, I might have selected him as well, just for laughs.

There are others that, throughout the year, some segments of our society raise to the level of worthy admiration. Among them was a deserter from the American military, who most recently attracted public attention. He escaped to Canada to avoid "having to kill people" in a war—at this moment, specifically the one in Iraq. I suspect, when he signed up for the armed forces, he assumed that before each battle the commanders would request a show of hands from their troops, to establish the worthiness of an upcoming action.

Don't misunderstand me. I was all in favour of draft-dodging Americans, who escaped during the war in Vietnam. Eventually many of them became "our kind" of Canadians. But this chap had volunteered for the forces; and his desertion from the military, to avoid killing or being killed, was an act that should be vigorously discouraged.

Another dubious case, in my unenlightened opinion, concerns the praise bestowed upon the former Canadian military leader of the U.N. contingent in Rwanda. He was the man on the spot at the time of their local genocide. A book he wrote about his experiences is a best-seller, but hardly the type of literature that would arouse my interest. Reports allege that he returned from his tour of duty, totally shattered by the "horrors of war" that he had witnessed. Ultimately he did get some reward. The prime minister of the day made him a senator, which places him, almost for eternity, into this rather dubious but still surviving political institution.

If questioned about my greatest hero, I could respond easily. Winston Churchill gets the vote. Perhaps it is because of my acquired commitment as an Anglophile, that I chose this saviour of "our" mother country. It could also be that since, in addition to his brilliance in getting Britain through the war, he—whenever throughout his lifetime he had again "gotten smarter"—occasionally changed his views dramatically. And his affliction with some shortcomings among his personal traits made him very human and brought him still closer to my heart.

As Canadian over-achievers I would quickly select the inventors and designers of our Avro Arrow aircraft, which made us world-leaders, until the politicians messed it up; the Banting/Best team of doctors that brought us Insulin and a better life to many sufferers of diabetes; and Pierre Berton, whose fascinating writings made us aware and proud of so much of our history. I would also include the entrepreneurial management and every last one of the exploited coolies involved in the construction of our transcontinental railway that helped to make our country. In this instance I even applaud the politicians of the time, who brought it about or at least allowed it to happen.

For the Canadian contingent, I would bypass the likes of Alexander Graham Bell and others frequently mentioned by our media as "Canadian achievers"; since, judged by the claims of some foreign jurisdictions, they might not easily qualify as our very own talent.

At the opposite end of the success spectrum, my listing of Canadian under-achievers would almost entirely be from the field of politics—with few notable exceptions. But, admittedly, theirs has never been an easy task; particularly with a client-base as critically demanding as I am.

TO THE PRIME MINISTER

With a new leadership of the team in Ottawa; an entirely different government for Ontario; and the possibility—I dare say, my sincere hope, which was since fulfilled—for a dramatic change of our national government after the next election; I wrote to the newly-anointed Prime Minister of Canada; to the Leader of our Official Opposition as Prime-Minister-in-waiting; and to the fully established Premier of Ontario.

With a differing introduction, of course, and slight variations in the order and the description of some of the items, the message was as follows:

For consideration by the political operatives in your office, these are my simple yet daring proposals (some might view them as overly simplistic).

A few of these recommendations fall into the sphere of provincial or territorial jurisdictions. Yet encouragement from federal authorities might facilitate their implementation by the junior governments as well.

Ethics Commissioner: Candidates for position, with one each proposed by the political parties, to be elected by Parliamentarians in a free "secret ballot" vote.

Governor General: To coincide with the end of the reign of our current Monarch, consider alternatives for a Canadian Head of State.

Lieutenant Governors: As a minimum adjustment, eliminate comparable positions of such royal representatives in Provincial jurisdictions.

Senate: Chosen by the electorate of each Province.

Voting: Restrict party membership; participation in candidates' nomination meetings; and the actual voting; to Canadian citizens only. Increase voter participation by enabling voting on-the-web.

Military: Convert entirely to a "Global Police Force" as peace-makers and peace-enforcers (rather than just peace-keepers).

Illegal Immigrants: Leave them with the delivering airlines for immediate return to their flight's point of origin.

Refugee Claimants: Accept none arriving from "safe" countries, no matter what their other citizenship or place of origin.

Sponsored Immigrants: Approve as sponsors only those capable of providing financial support; enforce their responsibility for their wards; deport protégés abandoned by their sponsors; provide federal reimbursement of provincial and municipal expenses where accrued.

Citizenship: No second citizenship of another country for Canadians.

Aborigines: Provide incentives for full integration into Canadian society.

National Identity Card: Introduce with photograph, fingerprints, and other technically possible identification.

Schools: Support only public schools; no tax benefits for contributors to private schools; no university admission for graduates without a standardized national high-school-graduation test.

French or English as Second Language: Continue support.

Foreign Aid: Cease for non-democratic countries.

Multiculturalism: Terminate government financial support.

Affirmative Action Quotas: Abolish.

Health Coverage: Provide services for Canadian "away from home" travellers within all our Provinces and Territories.

Hospitalization: Charge patients a daily fee.

Doctor Visits: Have patients pay a basic fee.

Prescription Drugs: Increase user fee service charge.

Canada Pension Plan: Raise contribution amounts and increase benefits paid.

RRSP Contribution: Increase limits.

Subsidies for the Underprivileged: Replace the many social benefits with a guaranteed minimum income.

Business Subsidies: Negotiate internationally to have these eliminated by all competing countries along with our own.

Service Fees: Privatize delivery and charge at least the true cost of administration for documents and licenses.

Fuel Taxes, Vehicle Registrations, Road Tolls, Parking Fees: Finance road construction and subsidies for public transportation from these.

Capital Gains Tax: Abolish.

GST/PST: Expand to all products and services; reduce general rate accordingly; and always include in the total sales price quoted.

Tax Rates: Base on combined household income.

Religious Properties and Institutions: Charge full real estate and "business" taxes.

Employment Insurance: Adjust rates regularly to recover the benefits paid and their administration.

Public Transport: Subsidize to increase the use by making it financially attractive.

Speed Limits: Raise these to a "reasonable" level (130 km/hr on four-lane high-ways) and then enforce them; at construction sites post meaningful speed reductions (only during the times when actually required) and then strictly enforce them.

Photo Radar: For safety, and not as a money-maker, provide permanent installa-tions for dangerous locations (intersections; curves; lane reductions); also have movable temporary checks at construction or accident sites.

Drug Use: Completely ignore the users; concentrate resources on dealers, with crim-inal charges equivalent to those for attempted murder.

Guns: Register hand-guns and automatic weapons only (with fees compensating for all costs of the program administration); add minimum 10 years to sentences for any criminal offence with a firearm.

Jail/Penitentiary Sentences: Only for crimes of violence (including drug dealing and child molestation). Occupy inmates with physical labour to pay for their upkeep.

Fines for other crimes and violations: Determine these as a percentage of an offender's income or wealth; or assign to work-gangs or community services as an alter-native to paying.

Ethnic/Religious Clashes: Deport non-Canadian participants whenever violence is committed.

Sexual Child Abuse: Castration and life-time incarceration.

Repeat Rape Offenders: Castration.

Water and Hydro Use: Charge users the market price or the actual cost of produc-tion.

Illegal Strikes: Recover cost from offenders.

Essential Service Strikes: Prohibit; settle disputes with a formula based on agree-ments reached by comparable groups in non-essential industries.

Charitable Programs: Charge organizers for cost of policing and for the clean-up services after an event (for parades, concerts, runs).

There could be more. For now, I am awaiting your reaction.

From a financial perspective, several of these suggestions could adversely affect me personally as well. So be it!

Optimistically yours,
(signed)

Responses differed greatly. The office of then-Prime Minister Paul Martin replied immediately. With a form letter, only slightly personalized, they acknowl-edged receipt and their full consideration. I suspect that—at the time of writ-ing—they had not yet read beyond the introduction to my submission, nor any intention of ever doing so.

The provincial Premier Dalton McGuinty provided no response at all. Even after my second submission, there was no reaction from his office. How did they know that I never voted for them? No doubt from the tone of my rightwing presentation.

The Office of the Leader of the Official Opposition responded for Stephen Harper, who shortly thereafter became Prime Minister. They went beyond a mere courteous acknowledgement, when they addressed not only the tone and intent, but indeed the content of several of my suggestions. Good on them! As my soul brothers, they might start with implementations, now that they have become the government!

CAREER GRANDPA

When I retired on August 19th 1993, the most appreciated of a number of mementos that my associates gave me was a sweatshirt. It showed the smiling face of Steven—at that time my only grandson—and the inscription "CAREER GRANDPA". It conveyed my views about retirement in a nutshell!

One of many pursuits to enjoy with our third generation in Canada, is for me to accompany our offspring during annual "bonding trips". With Steven, the eldest, we commenced this practice when he was not yet eight years old. Our first venture took us to *Disney World* in Orlando/Florida, where *a good time was had by all.*

"Whenever and wherever you want to travel, Grandpa, I will always go with you" is what he told me after we returned. Of course, he had been a world-traveller with his parents, ever since he was a baby. We recently tallied his many flights, among which he had already experienced 28 (twenty-eight!) transatlantic crossings.

I came to recognize and appreciate Steven as an ideal travel companion. And as soon as we returned from one of our ventures, I began planning for the next joint undertaking. Since Gussie no longer considers extensive tours as one of her favourite pastimes, I do live in anticipation of future one-on-one travels with grandchildren, during which I can then devote my entire attention to either one of the three darlings.

When it became Kevin's turn to accompany me on his own, he was quite hesitant. "No way will I travel without my Mommy", was his initial reaction. Then, all of a sudden, he, too, became keenly interested to accompany Grandpa. This commitment had to be explored to be verified. That's why, for Kevin's first venture with me, it seemed appropriate to have his older brother along as well. It also appeared preferable to go by car into the not-too-distant environment, just in case!

Kevin passed the test as a fellow-traveller. Then, by age eight, he was indeed ready for his very own solo expedition with me. And to Disney we went, just as I had done with his older brother, when he was the same age.

The only stressful part during any of these trips is always during my companions' daily enjoyment of the indoor pools, at the various hotels where we stay. All our grandchildren swim rather well, a talent which I never acquired. Whenever there are no lifeguards, I have to reach a "stand-by in an emergency" agreement with an adult swimmer, who uses the pool at the same time. Until this is confirmed, both Steven and Kevin confine their aquatic adventures to the shallow end. We also arranged that, if either one does any extended diving, one hand is frequently to be pointed above the water, to signal for me that everything is copasetic. Yet despite these precautions, I am never completely relaxed until they vacate the pool.

With our youngest, Emma, I may be beyond the adventurous travel stage when she gets to be old enough to accompany me. And it would indeed be a miracle, if I could endure long enough to participate in a family gathering for the wedding of a grandchild. Should I—against all odds—survive that long, I might not have retained all my marbles to provide any commentary. Even if galloping senility has not yet caught up with me by then, I could be challenged with my reading or speaking or just my staying-awake facilities. This is why I wanted to prepare some musings, from which one or the other point, suitable for a *brief* presentation, could be extracted.

For several generations, the Duerrs have ended up in "mixed marriages". My parents were raised with different religions; my father was also a big-city-kid while my mother had grown up in a small community. Gussie and I, of conflicting religions as well, had furthermore been strongly influenced by the philosophically contrasting—even antagonistic—milieus of the Prussian and the Southern German environments of our childhood. Our only son Ken and his spouse Birte ended up with a diverse heritage as well, their differing languages and citizenships. Although this was not a first in our lineage, since there were both French and Swiss nationals who had infiltrated the Germans among my early ancestors.

It would be up to my grandchildren to introduce—for the first time that we become aware of it—spouses of another race. Their mates could well come from Chinese, Persian, or South-American-Indian heritage—communities that were greatly "cultured", when our own forebears might still have roamed Europe as camp-followers of their barbarian tribes.

This could then be the family's contribution to a "melting pot" for our Canadian civilization—something I would favour greatly. I much prefer such evolution to our own government's struggle to preserve what they label a "multicultural *mosaic*". To me it is nothing but "*multicult apartheid*", an—albeit much more benign—promulgation of the former South African system that the so-called *civilized world* had been criticizing forever.

From my earlier writings, it should have become obvious, how I would prefer my descendants to progress. Certainly as Canadians and within what I perceive as our established *Leitkultur*—at least I thought this was our leading traditional culture when I made the then Dominion of Canada my country of choice. This society encompassed British traditions; Judean-Christian morals; and a bilingualism that consisted of English *and French*—to the exclusion of other "foreign" lingoes.

Who knows, among the future generations of our very own off-spring might well be someone committing to a same-sex marriage, something that governments at all levels are presently in the process of legalizing. At times it appears to me that liberal and socialist organizations, and much of the media, enthusiastically promote it as "an alternate lifestyle". And why not! It would not be my choice or my recommendation for any of my progeny. But, if so determined by their preferences, who am I to be critical of such a liaison, as long as the cohabitants turn out to be happy.

How can one predict the success or failure of any relationship? Commercial, personal or spiritual, all partnerships eventually reveal surprises—both pleasant and some not so pleasant—after they have been consummated. Arrangements that appear to have been "made in heaven", do not always work out; and others, assessed as doomed to failure from the start, can evolve into something really magnificent.

The gurus—many with their own failed relationships—advise inquisitive clients, who buy their books and videos or view their programs on the tube. They usually stress the obvious. Mutual respect, financial responsibility, sexual compatibility and—what I always considered the most significant component of an enduring relationship—a personal friendship, are basic requirements. It also helps if at least one of the partners is charmingly patient or has a great sense of humour. And then there is the mystique of *true love*, an enthrallment that defies rational definition.

We should all be so fortunate, to share this many mutual bonds! Some of us, miraculously, get it right from the start. Others improvise, make adjustments as required, and—eventually—live "happily ever after". Then there are those who—after what I've always termed a *trial* marriage—give up and, occasionally, try again. Not necessarily with more success the second time around.

My commentary should neither encourage nor discourage any of my descendants who consider entering the state of matrimony. It merely reflects what has been my experience, witnessing the efforts leading to the occasional "total bliss" among my contemporaries. Yet no matter how auspiciously splendid or awesomely challenging the situation looks at the start, it is no prediction on how it will develop over the initially planned time frame "until death do us part".

From all my writings, and—more significantly—from my conduct in my relationship with my three grandchildren throughout my lifetime so far, one thing should be obvious. I do love them dearly. It is with great pride that I relentlessly observe their progress in life. Constantly I recognize my good fortune, to be part of our wonderful family. I do hope that we will all be able to maintain our blessed state of relatively good health and happiness. And my sincere desire is for this to continue, with me, too, as "one of the players", for many years to come.

Daft and Dire Predictions

Since much of my original writing was intended for the amusement—perhaps the "enlightenment"—of my grandchildren and for their eventual off-spring, I wonder how they, or anyone else reading this, might relate to the concerns that one had at the beginning of the 21st century. My eldest grandson just turned fifteen. When he or his siblings have grandchildren of their own, and these reach the state where they can read my recollections, they may consider what I compose with this article today as pure hallucination.

My continually nurtured veneer of conceit has never reached the presumptuousness of considering myself a great creative thinker. Yet, occasionally, I do have strong deep thoughts of my very own, or expand knowledgably on the original views of others.

I read a fair bit and listen attentively to *talking heads* on television. Many commentators I reject because—as I see them—they are just spouting off words without conviction; they even lack the detailed knowledge of their subject. Others, with their professed sage musings, relate banalities that have already become obvious, even to the intellectually deprived. Those of a third group—again in my biased opinion—while reporting sensibly on a complicated theme, merely repeat ad nauseam what some real innovators had previously developed.

You will certainly not be able to complain to me if—some fifty years from now—these prophecies of mine have not materialized. Yet you may find it amusing to discover with what and by how much I have been wrong.

Here I go with my predictions for the future!

Excessive birth rates and an archaic social and economic environment in much of the third world will still leave their inhabitants hungry, poor, uneducated, diseased, and antagonistic towards the industrialized countries.

Their embezzling leaderships and corrupt elites will continue to pocket the only local wealth and much of the foreign aid to their deprived regions.

Masses of underprivileged global migrants will overrun the G7, even the wealthier of the other OECD countries, and flood them with their first and second generations' excessive birth rates.

The very low birthrate of those already established in today's Western civilizations will make Caucasians a mere minority in their former home countries.

China, Europe, India and North America will be the major international economies; with multinational companies determining the political and social agendas of most countries.

The permanently unemployable will reach a quarter of the defined work force; yet in the developed world, the normal working life will extend beyond seventy years of age.

Islam will be the most predominant of the *practiced* religions in Canada and the U.S.A.; many Protestant Christian denominations will have merged or disappeared; the Roman Catholic Church will have lost much of its influence.

Medical advances will have eradicated AIDS, West Nile Virus and much of Cancer in the developed world; the simple use of medications will replace surgical abortions.

Marijuana will have been decriminalized yet, along with the smoking of tobacco, will continue as an addiction of mouth-breathing lowbrows in "enlightened" societies, as well as among most of the impoverished in the third world.

Law enforcement resources will finally focus on the producers and distributors rather than on the users of illegal hard drugs.

While the "Singapore solution" would help eradicate the use of hard drugs and curtail the illegal use of guns, our authorities will still not implement the death penalty for drug dealers, nor the punishment of those committing crimes while using firearms with imprisonment for life.

Sentencing for non-violent crimes will no longer entail incarceration.

Significantly higher tax allocations will continue to finance comprehensive health care and expand to all levels of higher education in Canada.

Our publicly financed school systems will merge into one—and only one—non-denominational structure; religious teachings of any kind and other private education will be at the expense of the users.

Problems in the Middle East will remain unresolved.

The Islamist's struggle, to establish themselves as a global power, will continue through terrorism.

Lengthy security checks at transportation terminals and the continuing fear of disasters will significantly hinder long-distance travel.

Some of Canada's provinces will have merged into The West; The Prairies; Ontario; Quebec; and The Maritimes.

The predominant language of business in Quebec will be English.

Women will surpass with income and outperform men in many positions of importance; yet despite their achieved equality—even superiority—in a competitive environment, the self-anointed spokespersons for women and for visible minorities will persist in their whining about discrimination.

Aborigines, as they remain on reservations, will continue to be predominant among the most deprived of our compatriots.

And—now I am hopefully just being sarcastic—the federal Liberals will continue to have been in power over most of the time.

Long dead, cremated and—albeit not buried—spread into the wind myself, I hope to still amuse my descendants when they read my autobiographical dissertations.

Not an Apology

Perhaps it was more than a mere joke and a gentle hint. It could have been a message of real significance, when our kids presented me with a t-shirt inscribed *Warning: Retiree—Knows it all and has plenty of time to tell you about it.*

It's been a while since anyone asked me seriously for professional advice. Occasionally, a former associate might—as I sometimes suspect—just try to humour me, when inquiring about my previous work environment. Since I severed all contact with the organization and with anyone still employed there on the day when I retired more than ten years ago, there isn't anything I can divulge that might still be relevant for the current organization.

I am, however, in frequent contact with several former colleagues, who are either retired as well or, since my departure, have taken on different assignments in other work areas. Yet seldom do our conversations stray into the "remember when?" domain.

At times, friends from my private surroundings do me the honour, when seeking my views on aspects of their life's personal and professional challenges. When I respond to the best of my ability, I really don't know if any of the observations I relay will then prove useful. My advice might be just as dangerously misleading as the "hot tips" one regularly encounters for investments.

I act quite differently within my immediate family. I do not just *respond*; I *initiate* without even the slightest encouragement! I find it difficult—if not impossible—to successfully stifle my keen interest in the endeavours of those really close to me, and to curtail my youthful enthusiasm to provide some pearls of wisdom. Whenever I have dispensed another unsolicited bit of "sage counsel", I recall with consternation my prior serious intent to provide such commentary *exclusively* in response to *specific requests*. It seems that I never learn!

This is a different world; and all a retired person—I cringe when being tagged as "elderly", although it might be quite appropriate in my case—allegedly knows is about *them olden days.* Today the generational gap is just as immense as it was between me and my father—however, not as pronounced with my mother—half a century ago; and Ken and Birte will observe the same as their own children mature.

Fortunately, perhaps, my parents never commented as much *to me* regarding my intended doings, as I constantly do directly to my offspring about their planned actions. At times my folks must have been equally interested or intrigued. Yet had they voiced their opinion, I could well have considered this as an intrusion.

I was no exception with my normal reaction to "the preceding generation", so why should our offspring be any different. You do not learn much from the mistakes of others. You have to make your own and then, hopefully, you will have a useful recollection, when you again encounter a similar challenge in the future. Above all, though, who knows what is right or wrong or better or best; particularly in other time periods and different environments.

There were a fair number of daring actions that I—in my *small-c* conservative way—would have counselled our kids against. Yet, despite my apprehensions, many of these choices turned out to be splendidly successful.

When I pass along some sagacious advice to my grandchildren, they, despite their young age, detect as well that my disclosures can not always prove authentic. For emphasis, Gussie or I may recount an earlier experience that we had with our son. We might comment to them that their father frequently accomplished this or that, or never ever would have done such and such. Occasionally it is our son himself, who then reveals to his children, and surprisingly to us, that we "have it all wrong". Since—we never would have thought it at the time—he really was involved in some dubious projects, without our awareness and beyond our imagination. Yet, to the best of our current knowledge, none of Kenneth's actions ever qualified as the type of delinquency, which I described in a previous book as some of my own childhood misdeeds.

When they are in my charge, the members of the third generation of Canadian Duerrs seem to have no difficulties in doing things somewhat differently from their normal routines. To have them conform to my constraints, they occasionally receive directives rather than mere advice. I tell them "you are temporarily under new management". Then, for the duration of our close encounters—be it for mere hours on a shared undertaking, or for a week or more during our joint travels—my grandchildren don't even seem to mind, when drinking either juice or milk or water *instead* of pop, which obligatory substitutions result from just one of my everlasting edicts.

Gussie has always been much more reserved than I will ever become. She observes but generally abstains from "suggestions of the interfering kind"; while I compulsively see it as my role to proffer advice with the heartfelt intent to be helpful. Often, I can then portray an experience of my own, which might parallel the novel scheme to be approached by our young ones.

I really try to control or at least limit my involvement—unless it has been specifically requested. However, aware of my keen interest and great concern for everything to do with my offspring, to *cease and desist* completely may prove an impossible task.

Whenever, with great gusto, I "fall off the wagon", our kids will recognize that I had only the very best of intentions. And for these I need not apologize.

READING CAN BE FUN

As long as I can remember, I have always been an avid reader. My parents tried to stifle some of this excessive enthusiasm, to allow me more time to focus on school work. I specifically recall one incident.

From my limited pocket money, I had saved enough to buy an adventure story "*Tom Mix der Held* (hero) *von Texas*"—no doubt a topic not acceptable by my father's standards. As soon as I brought it into the house, he burned it in our wood-stove. My frenzied reaction—followed by days of sulking—precluded any recurrence of such a drastic solution This experience still comes to mind, whenever I encounter one of the more significant book-burnings in my historical discoveries.

My father also found it necessary to curtail my reading late at night, to provide me with a good night's sleep before the next day's schooling. Since frequent reminders to shut off the light brought no results, he at times removed the fuses and thereby cut off the electricity into my room. Occasionally I was still able to continue my reading with the use of a flashlight.

Much of my limited wealth as a youngster went into the acquisition of books. Very few of these I had been able to bring to Canada, when—during another visit to Germany—I was astounded to learn that all my remaining possessions had been given away. By then it was too late to remedy this debacle.

I always preferred to *purchase* the worthier volumes that particularly interested me. Only new books, that is; with acquisitions from garage sales, even previously unread bargains, an absolute no-no. Once my very own, they were cherished and protected and *never* lent out to anyone else for reading. I have relented just a little on this recently, but restricted the circulation to really "trustworthy"—meaning *careful with my property*—individuals.

In recent months (not days but *months*) I have endured the series by J. K. Rowling. Her latest creation has over 600 pages. This much extended period to peruse *any* bulky tome has two causes. I usually read more than just one book at a time; and with such physically unwieldy hard-cover editions, I need even more of the usual interruptions for a respite. The second cause for the delay is, of course, that—with gradually deteriorating eye sight—my speed-reading days seem to be over. My optometrist tells me that I have not yet reached the stage for a cataract operation. This leaves me to occasionally struggle, while absorbing but one word at a time.

When I still worked for a living, my literary exploits were primarily job-related. If I found time for recreational reading, I preferred adventurous paperbacks with historical fiction—or fictionalized history—by authors such as Tom Clancy, James Clavell, Günter Grass, Arthur Hailey, James Michener, Edward Rutherfurd or Leon Uris.

Since my retirement, I am primarily into *history*, ancient as well as current, which often confirms that we don't really learn from our mistakes; into *religion*, just to discover what makes others tick, and certainly not in search of salvation; and into current *politics*, mainly to reaffirm my prejudicial disillusionment about many of the players.

Yet I also enjoy the exploration of "need to know" subjects on home repair; gardening; wildlife; health; investing; which I seek out consistently. What I don't find in books, I glean from magazines and newspapers, or search on the web.

I don't think I spend much more than twenty minutes reviewing the morning paper. I glance at all the headlines; peruse the content of items of particular interest; yet skip the actual articles on everything that I have previously ascertained from radio or television news.

Commentary I review consistently is in editorials, particularly those presenting views opposing my own; the observations by financial gurus and their unconvincing predictions for the market or certain stocks; the local weather to determine how it differs from radio and television forecasts; and the obituary columns, seeking reassurance that I am not mentioned.

Recalling another pronouncement by Winston Churchill—although it must have been used in an entirely different context—his "This is the kind of writing up with which I will not put" makes me abstain completely from letters to the editor. They are as bad as the phone-in programs on radio. I also ignore reports on local crime, fire and accident information; I quickly activate the mute-button when these are mentioned during TV newscasts. I have no need for stock prices, since I can view these more currently on the web. And I successfully tune out all advertisements and anything else from which I already suffer over-exposure.

When Kenneth was little, Gussie and I went through the usual highly recommended routine—Dr. Spock was the authority at the time—of reading to our son. Once he commenced his schooling, we provided material and encouraged his literary exploits. This has not been a lasting success since, as I observe today, he seems to limit himself primarily to must-read material that relates to his profession—even more restrictive than I ever did during my career.

For our grandchildren, I am still with great expectations for their evolution as bookworms. As Birte suggests, and I previously mentioned in another context, sometimes such traits "skip a generation". One of the three sweethearts might well get to be as enthusiastic a reader as I am; or as their mother is as well, although to a lesser degree.

WRITING FOR PROFIT

When my spouse discovered that I was planning to write another book, this current one, she again wondered why—and this time she did it aloud. Why, indeed, would I continue to publish these volumes at continuing expense to myself, instead of with a financial return like that of "other authors", she enquired. Gussie clearly overestimates my literary talents.

I am old enough to have encountered a Pierre Berton—his many volumes of *Canadiana* are among my favourites—or some of our other commercially rewarded writers; and I live in a region of the country, where many from Canada's literary elite reside. Yet I never even saw these guys in person nor, to the best of my knowledge, any other *successful* authors. And I realistically gauge that I am not their kind of gifted writer, either.

Could it be this inadequate literary skill, or my insignificant personage—performing as both the primary hero and major villain in my very own yarns—that hamper the creation of a widely adoring readership? Surely such limitations impede commercial triumph beyond a circle of family and friends.

I vaguely recall someone's astounding comment, concerning the still bestselling *DaVinci Code*. If one could believe such a reproachful critic in his attack of the immensely victorious Dan Brown, this author and I seem to have at least one thing in common. In the opinion of the envious, his works, too, are allegedly "badly written". Of course, his presentations—which I enjoyed greatly—continue to be promoted through the frequent condemnation of his purportedly blasphemous insinuations. With the berating outbursts that they bestow on him, the Christian churches' faithful inadvertently guarantee his ever-increasing sales.

In response to a question that has not yet been asked, but must certainly occur to you: No, I am *not* fishing for compliments, whenever I belittle my struggles with these whimsical asides. I merely express, once again, my frequently demonstrated self-deprecating humour. But I eagerly anticipate any serious critique, since this will stir me to do more—hey, who knows, perhaps even better—writing.

I have no hesitation to freely admit some of my eccentricities as an aspiring writer. Offsetting segments of my lines with hyphens—as I do in this instance—is one of my annoying habits; at times, so I suspect, I even speak this way. I start sentences with "And" as well as "But", which the *literati* consider inappropriate. My commas and semi-colons appear in a most wondrous array. I usually place them according to German norm, which I was taught in grade school; or let myself be guided by "a feeling" about their appropriateness. They may not always be in accordance with precise rules, the knowledge of which—for the English language—I never acquired. Following paragraphs may not be segued to the preceding text. Verbose is how I personally assess some of my phrases; repetitive and long-winded the occasional description that I compose. One can also accuse me of the sporadic application of a highfalutin word, which, to avoid sounding pompous in my speech, I intentionally shun in everyday dialogue. But, surely, I can expect the distinguished group of my enraptured readers to be appreciative of a more sophisticated vocabulary.

Meanings of unfamiliar foreign-language terms, generally in Danish, French or German, become obvious within the surrounding text. The rare mutation of something I personalized from *The Queen's English*, might not yet have qualified for entry in a *Dictionary of Canadian English*. My message to you on these unorthodox expressions: Listen up and (perhaps?) learn something!

Always keenly interested to study my surroundings, I amassed knowledge—both useful and superfluous—from seven decades' worth of wide-ranging observations; some obviously also came from reading books. This let me acquire broad perspectives and strong opinions about many of the challenges that faced the world throughout my existence, as well as on the problems that confront us today.

In this volume, an occasional "pearl of wisdom"—where not my very own innovative thought—might have been impossible to relate to its original source. If and when an author, of the infinite number of readings I enjoyed over the years, discovers something in my own musings, for which he or she should have been credited, the fully functioning compartment of my brain apologizes. The originating commentator should be flattered that my mind retained the information over so many years; even if, in another segment of my intellect, I failed to connect my own contemplation to the thought's precise origin. Otherwise I would surely have bestowed a well-deserved honourable mention on the instigator. Surely no such omission could deprive someone of their well-deserved royalties!

On the expenditure angle of my own presentations, it is only our kids, if anyone at all, who should be concerned with the cost of producing my continuing observations; or the dearth of financial returns from their sales. After all, they will be the ones who eventually end up with our thereby diminished remaining loot.

Several of my friends are "into writing" as well. Their projects range from the autobiographical, like my own; to interpretations of historical events, vaguely related to their personal experiences; to adventurous fiction, for the creation of which I lack the imagination; to children's books, something I, too, might want to explore some day.

None of my fellow-writers *really* need the money from profitable sales; most just strive—still unsuccessfully—to have something in print at all. Others paid for their self-publications; one chap I know is presently into his twelfth volume. Despite an occasional "paying customer", I suspect that all these triumphant releases continue to entail a financial deficit.

Researching on the internet, I discovered a number of websites trying to convince me that, using their promoters as intermediaries, I would quickly become a success. Oh yeah? One of these, for free, provided me with a diagnostic verdict on one of my stories. Full of praise for my *obvious talents*—the italics are mine, the words were theirs—they recommended that I submit to their personalized tutoring, specifically attuned to my very own requirements. This would then have made me even more polished, with great success in literary circles—for a fee, of course.

Not to leave any ambiguity about my prospects as one of their paying customers, I promptly advised them of my decision not to enrol. Yet, just the same, I am still on their mailing list for continuous reminders, to join their distinguished clientele. They must really feel that, with an enlarged readership—which their teachings could almost (but not quite) *guarantee*—the exposure to my creations would contribute greatly to the cultural edification of my fellow-man.

Even without commercial success, I am certain that my friends the "fellow-authors", as I do, derive what must be narcissistic gratification from their handouts. Just like blogging, this could even be therapeutic. You might like to try it some day! As hobbies go, there could indeed be worse things to occupy your time than struggling as a still unsuccessful author. Don't you agree?

EPILOGUE

It may be apparent from some of my commentary, that I can be persuaded to change my mind. Following the presentation of facts, my biased perspective of the universe, and how it does, or, how it *should* evolve, can be revised—albeit thereby not necessarily improved. Since I am less able to change my biases, they remain as the lens through which I view our world; although I strive to keep facts and biases in their proper place.

One inevitably becomes more knowledgeable with advancing years. Yet one's associates, particularly the younger ones, do not always recognize such enhancement as being positive. What is offered as sage commentary based on a lengthy association with the world, is easily passed off as the muttering of a know-it-all, or worse, an old fool.

Opsimathy is the rather ostentatious name for education late in life. I do not know if such sophisticated terminology could apply to me, for the many talents that I acquired since my retirement. Among them—one of my more frequently practiced "skills"—is the continuing creation of autobiographical books, for which this yarn becomes the final insert in the latest volume.

Scrutiny of all my writings might well expose certain inconsistencies that evolved in my views over time. This provides proof that I remain open to new revelations, and that I have used the experience that comes with age to interpret such facts differently. Could I possibly be getting smarter? Presumptuous of me to declare this to be obvious, eh!

I want to give but one example. It concerns my instructions concerning the disposal of my earthly remains—now there is a cheerful thought—once I have succumbed to the ravages of age. I was quite categorical with my earlier direction, that there should be no memorial service of any kind. As quickly as possible after my demise, with absolutely no fanfare and ensuring the least possible expense, I want to be cremated. Yet, for the ritual thereafter, I could now be swayed when it comes to the eventual disposal of the ashes.

My father and mother were cremated. Their urns are in a *Columbarium* at the cemetery in Karlsruhe, the city where I was born. They died in 1974 and 1982 respectively. Despite my earlier decree about the unceremonious discarding of my own ashes, a visit to my parents' burial site is always the first thing I do, when I visit the area. This lets me "pay my respects" and quietly reflect for a little while, upon their impact on me and on my own life.

Cremation is never part of a Jewish funeral routine, as I am led to believe. However, I discovered one of their customs that, instead of flowers, some mourners bring little pebbles to place at the gravesite. I find this ritual most admirable. As the result, whenever I visit Karlsruhe, I take along and deposit at the family burial site a small stone from my garden, from the farm, or from the family's cottage.

It recently occurred to me that, with my strong emotional attachment to my ancestors' final resting place, my descendants might develop similar idiosyncrasies, and come to appreciate an equally revered place of remembrance. Unless, of course, they turn out to be not quite as sentimental as I am, in which case to "spread my ashes in the wind" would still be fine with me.

BIBLIOGRAPHY

Throughout a reasonably long life, I read many hundreds of books; observed even more commentators; viewed thousands of articles; and had an immense number of exchanges with family, friends, educators, colleagues, clients, even with total strangers. Based on these at times highly valued contributions, and my very personal experiences in "the book of life", I amassed data, acquired knowledge and formed the opinions that are reflected in my writings.

To commence with an entirely new volume, on something as precise as "Henry Ford and his Model-T", or "John Diefenbaker and our Avro-Arrow", I could research each subject in dozens of books and on hundreds of websites. Listing the more pertinent ones in a *Bibliography* segment would then be an easy task.

There was no need to search for new wisdom, when I composed these autobiographical revelations. Yet, although fully amassed in my cranium, I usually had no recollection of which component I might have gleaned from whom, and when and where. Even if able to attribute a specific thought to someone, I couldn't possibly recollect when I first became aware of this—nor, occasionally, guarantee that the assumed author and the alleged saying were *really* linked. There are but a couple of exceptions in this book, and for these I reveal my source within the text of the appropriate chapter.

Those of my friends, who have been a fountain of wisdom in our constant exchanges over the years, and could be prodded into an editorial review of some of these compositions, still prefer to remain anonymous. It must be the controversial nature of so much of what I have to say that makes them decline the honour of being identified. They know I appreciated their contributions, which I will acknowledge with my inscription in their very own copy of the finished product.

The result of all this is, of course, that my segment "Bibliography", with a total lack of the customary references, is as unconventional as so much else that I compose. Surely this can be understood—and forgiven.

978-0-595-42819-9
0-595-42819-3